What the Bible
Really Says about

LOVE,
MARRIAGE,
and
FAMILY

To
Dr. Jim Dyson
who,
with humor, patience,
and encouragement,
convinced me that God is,
and baptized me in Christ.

What the Bible
Really Says about

LOVE, MARRIAGE, and FAMILY

John Temple Bristow

Chalice Press
St. Louis, Missouri

Biblical quotations, unless otherwise noted, are from the *New Revised Standard Version Bible (with Apocrypha)*, copyright 1989, Division of Christian Education of the National Council of the Churches of Christ in the USA. Used by permission.

Those quotations marked RSV are from the *Revised Standard Version* of the Bible, copyrighted 1946, 1952, © 1971, 1973.

Those quotations marked NIV are taken from the Holy Bible, New International Version, copyright © 1978 by the New York International Bible Society. Used by permission of Zondervan Bible Publishers.

Cover illustration: Will Hardin
Art Director: Michael Dominguez

10 9 8 7 6 5 4 3 2 1

Library of Congress Cataloging–in–Publication Data

Bristow, John Temple.
    What the Bible really says about love, marriage, and family /
by John Temple Bristow.
      p. cm.
    ISBN 0-8272-4232-8
    1. Marriage—Biblical teaching. 2. Mate selection—Biblical teaching. 3. Sex—Biblical teaching 4. Woman (Christian theology)—Biblical teaching. 5. Divorce—Biblical teaching.
6. Family—Biblical teaching.   I. Title.
BS680.M35B75   1994
261.8'358'0901—dc20   94–11396

Printed in the United States of America

Preface

This work has grown out of what was originally a much larger manuscript, *How to Be Surprised by the Bible.* I want to express my deep appreciation to those who read and commented on that longer writing and helped me to extrapolate and focus my energies on a more manageable topic. I am especially grateful to Elaine and Phill Aney, Chuck Barnard, the late Eleanor Corbus, Charlotte Hillstead, Howard Hilzinger, Janet Hutchinson, Hazel Kraemer, Bob and Lucille Lee, Ingrid Lewison, Cathy and Gary McKee, Nancy McMurrer, George Mooney, Patty Protzeller, Gail and Richard Record, Melanie Sanayebakhsherad, Rita Seegrist, Betty and Homer Schmitt, Bob and Sally Sibson, Randy and Vicky Utterback, and Louise Van Poll. I am deeply indebted to them for their helpful responses.

I am also very appreciative of my wife, Christy Bristow, for her insightful comments and the use of her writing, "Sermon on the Rug." I also give special thanks for the encouragement I received from two pastors, Dr. Roger Cone and Christine Morton, from Patricia Emory, a Christian educator, and from Laura Gregg, a highly gifted group discussion leader.

In addition, I want to express my appreciation to the members of Murray Hills Christian Church (Disciples of Christ) who have offered to me, their new pastor, comments and suggestions concerning the variety of models of marriage presented in this study.

Contents

Introduction

This book is different than any other, offering a fresh view of the meaning of marriage and family life within the Bible. It is full of surprises, precisely because it does not presuppose that people in biblical times experienced marriage and home life in the same way as people do today.

Imagine Isaac, for example, restlessly awaiting the return of his father's servant from distant Ur, bringing with him a relative whom Isaac had never met, a woman who would become Isaac's wife and the mother of his children.

Picture Sarah, awake at night listening to her husband Abraham engaging in sexual intercourse with Sarah's servant, fer-

1

vently praying that he would impregnate Hagar so that she might bear Abraham and Sarah a son.

Consider a widow who had been given to her brother-in-law, so that he might produce an heir for her dead husband, and, when he too died, was given to yet another brother-in-law, and imagine that this happened repeatedly until she had married seven brothers in all! This was a hypothetical scenario presented to Jesus by some Sadducees, but it did reflect the real practice of levirate marriage, in which a woman might marry several men, all brothers, never once having been given a choice of who shared her bed or her body.

Sense the shock felt by Jesus' listeners when he told them that a man who did not "hate" his own family would not be worthy to become a disciple of Jesus. Picture Jesus taking little children up into his arms and blessing them, thereby dramatically ridiculing the time-honored patriarchal family structure.

In other words, expect this book to examine scripture passages concerning marriage and family life from a fresh perspective.

This book, therefore, asks that the reader be willing to be surprised. What is said in these pages reminds us that the Bible was not written with the twentieth or twenty-first centuries in mind, nor was it written to affirm our own culture today.

For example, the first two chapters present three different views on sexuality that underlie many Old Testament laws and customs: women as sexual property, sex as worship, and sex as a blessing from God.

Chapter 3 examines different motives for marriage and the variety of methods recorded in the Old Testament for selecting marriage partners.

The following two chapters identify seven different biblical models of marriage found in the Bible. Five of these, which have only indirect counterparts in modern Western society, are included in Chapter 4. The other two, both exemplified in Eden, are contrasted in Chapter 5.

The next two chapters focus upon the biblical ideal of marriage, that "the two shall become one flesh," with Chapter 6 exploring how Jesus used this strange wording as a basis for marriage and Chapter 7 examining how Paul used it as a basis for sexual morality. New Testament teachings about divorce are illuminated by their cultural context in Chapter 8.

Chapter 9 presents several surprising biblical concepts about family, including reasons why Jesus spoke so negatively about family relationships. The final chapter examines some difficult passages dealing with relationships between Christians and offers a charming example of how scriptures about relationships in general can be applied to family life. An appendix deals with the question of marriage in the life to come.

Readers of my first book, *What Paul Really Said About Women*, often tell me they appreciated being provided a list of discussion questions at the end of each chapter and having pertinent scripture passages printed out in full, so that they would not have to stop reading in order to look up biblical references. I have included both of these features in this volume.

Unless otherwise specified, all scripture quotations are taken from the *New Revised Standard Version Bible*.

One additional note: readers may notice that the treatment of scriptures in this book is somewhat different from that found in many other religious writings. Instead of simply lifting out and considering one or two verses at a time, I will examine passages of scripture in their context within the Bible and within their cultural setting. I will not utilize scriptures for their inspirational value, nor will I appeal to a traditional understanding of any particular portion of scripture simply because that understanding is old. In my experience, reading the Bible is far more rewarding if we put aside our own preconceptions of what a passage means and then strive to get inside the skins of biblical people and hear the words afresh.

In order to do this, it is helpful to ask three questions of any portion of scripture:

- Who would have understood this account best? Considering this helps us look at the passage from the perspective of its originally intended readers.

- Who would have been most shocked by this scripture? Many of the passages of the Bible were surprising—even offensive—to certain people. This is especially true of the Gospels, where almost every teaching of Jesus would have shocked some hearers and outraged others.

- What surprises await us from this passage? Even familiar scriptures sometimes startle us when we discover that they contain things we had failed to notice before or that they omit things we assume must be there. This third question urges us to engage the text with a frame of mind that allows room for new insights and fresh understandings.

—John Temple Bristow

1

Women as Sexual Property

Should a man protect his wife and children? If so, does this responsibility grant him the right to exercise some control over his wife's behavior as well as his children's? Does it grant him the right to regard his wife and children as—in some sense—his property?

Does a woman truly own her own body? If so, does this ownership grant her the right to make independent and absolute decisions regarding her reproductive abilities? Does it grant her more extensive parental rights over her children than those rights enjoyed by their father?

Many persons today, whether fundamentalists, evangelicals, liberals, or nonbelievers, are quietly confident that they know how the scriptures would answer these important questions—whether or not they personally agree with what they think the Bible says.

This confidence is seldom justified, simply because common words such as *marriage, wife, husband, family,* and *household* meant quite different things to people in biblical days than they mean to members of modern industrialized societies.

The problem of reading our own experiences into the Bible

Ernest Campbell once said that the Bible is like a mirror. "So if an ass looks in," he stated, "don't expect to find an apostle peering out." He has identified a serious problem with biblical study: our tendency to read our own thoughts and experiences into the text. Scholars call this process *eisogesis,* imposing our own ideas onto the scriptures.

In examining what the Bible really says about any topic we must carefully avoid projecting our own concepts onto the text. We must refrain from interpreting biblical words according to our own experiences and understanding. These prohibitions are absolute requirements for objective biblical study. Doing otherwise makes the Bible into a mirror instead of a source of wisdom and guidance.

In order to discover biblical insights about marriage and families, we must begin by setting aside any assumptions about masculine and feminine, love, matrimony, and family life. We must listen to the text humbly and attentively, without preconception or prejudice.

If we begin by assuming that people in biblical days held the same attitudes about sexuality that we do today, then we will become confused by scripture passages relating to marriage and families. Many of the customs and laws in the Bible will leave us puzzled, and we will be startled by many of its stories.

Instead, we will begin this study by asking two very basic questions: what did it mean to be male or female in the ancient

Near East, and, how did the people of biblical times regard sexual intimacy?

The concept of sexual property

Many laws and marriage practices in ancient Israel were based on one very important idea about sexuality: women as sexual property. Although both Jesus and Paul rejected this notion, leaders of the early church nonetheless re-affirmed the social standing of women as sexual property, as do numerous preachers today.

The concept is illustrated by a phrase that appears frequently in ancient literature, "women, slaves, children." In many societies during biblical times women were regarded as one of three classes of humans owned by others. Female children and female slaves were, in a sense, doubly owned.

It is essential that we understand this concept of sexual property if we are to make sense out of certain Mosaic laws regarding women and marriage, as well as numerous other Old Testament passages. For example, note the wording in the following curse:

> You shall become engaged to a woman, but another man shall lie with her. You shall build a house, but not live in it. You shall plant a vineyard, but not enjoy its fruit.
>
> Deuteronomy 28:30

The author of this passage placed a betrothed woman in the same category as a man's house or a man's vineyard. All three are a man's property, possessions that may be taken away from him.

Wives as sexual property

When Job protested his innocence and the unfairness of his suffering, he chose words that reflect the concept of wives as property of their husbands:

> If my heart has been enticed by a woman,
> and I have lain in wait at my neighbor's door;
> then let my wife grind for another,
> and let other men kneel over her.
>
> Job 31:9–10

Job was saying, in effect, "if I have stolen another man's wife, then let the same be done to me—let *my* wife be stolen." Job was not thinking of his wife as a person in her own right, with feelings and self-will. Instead, he spoke of her as an item of property, however precious that property might be. Setting aside the question of relative value, Job could have said much the same about his livestock as about his wife. He might just as well have stated, "if I have stolen another man's sheep, let my sheep be stolen."

Job's choice of words reflect the important fact that in ancient Hebrew society (and in other, neighboring cultures) girls were regarded as the property of their fathers and wives as the property of their husbands. This same attitude underlies a law found in Numbers 30:3–15 that defines how a woman's father or her husband might annul the vows she has made to God.

> When a woman makes a vow to the Lord, or binds herself by a pledge, while within her father's house, in her youth, and her father hears of her vow or her pledge by which she has bound herself, and says nothing to her; then all her vows shall stand, and any pledge by which she has bound herself shall stand. But if her father expresses disapproval to her at the time that he hears of it, no vow of hers, and no pledge by which she has bound herself, shall stand; and the Lord will forgive her, because her father had expressed to her his disapproval.
>
> Numbers 30:3–5

The law then states that a woman's husband shall have the same right of veto for any vow his wife might make.

Although this law permits a girl's father or a wife's husband to annul her sacred vows, at least it specifies that a widow or a divorced woman may make and keep such vows. In most other ways, however, a widow or a divorced woman in Hebrew society was granted very few rights and privileges, in that she did not belong to any man. This fact makes Jesus' parable about a widow who repeatedly confronted an unjust judge all the more remarkable. The same may be said for the early church's creation of a special ministry in which widows were honored and given special tasks to perform (1 Timothy 5:3–16).

Concubines as sexual property

The concept of women as sexual property shaped the history of Israel through its patriarchs and its kings.

In Genesis 35 we read of how Reuben, Jacob's eldest son, engaged in sexual intercourse with Jacob's concubine, Bilhah. Jacob knew of Reuben's violation of his father's sexual property. Although Jacob did not punish Reuben, he never forgot this son's offense.

As eldest son, Reuben would normally become the new patriarch after Jacob's death and rule over his brothers and their families. But Jacob refused to bequeath that status to Reuben. Instead, on his deathbed Jacob cursed Reuben:

> "Unstable as water, you shall no longer excel
> because you went up onto your father's bed;
> then you defiled it—you went up onto my couch!"
>
> Genesis 49:4

Jacob also disinherited his next two sons, Simeon and Levi, because they were men of violence. He bestowed his blessing instead upon Judah, making him the new patriarch over the family, saying, "your brothers shall praise you;…your father's sons shall bow down before you" (Genesis 49:8). This account foreshadows the preeminence of Judah among the other tribes and the eventual separation of the Northern Kingdom from Judah.

Bible readers often assume that concubines were the sexual property of their husbands because these women were also lowly slaves. However, the concubines of Israelite kings—intimate royal property—served as living symbols of royal power. Bedding such a concubine would be as much an act of rebellion as seizing the crown. Knowing this enables us to understand an otherwise puzzling event that helped establish the dynasty of King David.

Ishbaal, a son of King Saul, accused Abner, Saul's general, of having sexual relations with Rizpah, one of the king's concubines. Abner rightly regarded this as nothing less than an accusation of treason. He responded by swearing allegiance to David against Saul (2 Samuel 3:7ff), an important endorsement of David's eventual ascendancy to the royal throne.

Years later Absalom, one of David's sons, decided to declare a coup d'état against his father. Absalom was advised by his associate Ahithophel:

> "Go in to your father's concubines, the ones he has left to look after the house; and all Israel will hear that you have made yourself odious to your father, and the hands of all who are with you will be strengthened." So they pitched a tent for Absalom upon the roof; and Absalom went in to his father's concubines in the sight of all Israel.
>
> 2 Samuel 16:21–22

Another of David's sons, Adonijah, tried to use his father's concubine in a similar sexual/political manner. He had planned to have himself proclaimed the new king of Israel just as soon as David died. Bathsheba, however, heard of Adonijah's design. So she ran to David (who was on his deathbed) and persuaded him to name Solomon, her son, as his royal successor. After Adonijah learned of this, he chose to refrain from making any public challenge of David's statement. Instead, he sought to gain the throne by a more devious means. He sought the hand of David's last and most lovely concubine, Abishag.

> Then Adonijah son of Haggith came to Bathsheba, Solomon's mother. She asked, "Do you come peaceably?" He said, "Peaceably." Then he said, "May I have a word with you?" She said, "Go on." He said, "You know that the kingdom was mine, and that all Israel expected me to reign; however, the kingdom has turned about and become my brother's, for it was his from the LORD. And now I have one request to make of you; do not refuse me." She said to him, "Go on." He said, "Please ask King Solomon—he will not refuse you— to give me Abishag the Shunammite as my wife."
>
> 1 Kings 2:13–17

Bathsheba agreed to approach King Solomon on Adonijah's behalf. It is difficult to imagine that she did so without knowing full well what her royal son's response would be.

> The king rose to meet her, and bowed down to her; then he sat on his throne, and had a throne brought for the king's mother, and she sat on his right. Then she said, "I have one small request to make of you; do not refuse me." And the king said to her, "Make your request, my mother; for I will not refuse you." She said, "Let Abishag the Shunammite be given to your brother Adonijah as his wife." King Solomon answered his mother, "And why do you ask Abishag the Shunammite for Adonijah? Ask for him the kingdom as well! For he is my elder brother; ask not only for him but also for the priest Abiathar and for Joab son of Zeruiah!" Then King Solomon swore by the LORD, "So may God do to me, and more also, for Adonijah has devised this scheme at the risk of his life! Now therefore as the LORD lives, who has established me and placed me on the throne of my father David, and who has made me a house as he promised, today Adonijah shall be put to death." So King Solomon sent Benaiah son of Jehoiada; he struck him down, and he died.
>
> 1 Kings 2:19b–25

Being familiar with the concept of women as sexual property, then, enables us to understand how a violation of the concubine could lose Reuben his patrimony and Adonijah his life. A concubine was valuable not so much for who she was, but whose she was. If she belonged to the ruling patriarch or king, her actions may effect the course of a nation's history.

Adultery as a violation of property rights

The notion that women are sexual property explains why adultery, according to the law of Moses, was not regarded as a crime against the male offender's wife. Even though a wife was her husband's property, *he* was not *her* property. Therefore, although a wife might violate her husband's marital rights, he could not violate her marital rights—simply because she did not possess any such rights. A man could commit adultery, to be sure, but the victim—the only victim—was the adulterous partner's husband.

Hence, if a married man engaged in sexual intercourse with a unmarried woman, he was not guilty of adultery. But if a married woman engaged in sexual intercourse with an unmarried man, she was guilty of a capital offense.

If a man only suspected that his wife had been unfaithful to him, but had no proof, he might demand that her marital faithfulness be tested (Numbers 5:11–31). The priest would write down a curse against the woman, condemning her before God if she were secretly guilty of adultery. He would read this curse to her, set her before the tabernacle, and dishevel her hair. Then, taking a clay jar filled with holy water, the priest would pour into it both dust from the tabernacle floor and ashes from an offering of barley grain into it, thereby creating the "water of bitterness." After washing the written curse in this mixture, he would require the woman to drink it, warning her of the harm it would do her if she were guilty.

The "water of bitterness" was expected to induce an abortion of an illegitimate fetus and to prevent the woman from bearing any more children. The law of Moses described this ruthless form of psychological/medical testing in graphic detail:

> the water that brings the curse shall enter into her and cause bitter pain, and her womb shall discharge, her uterus drop, and the woman shall become an execration among her people....The man shall be free from iniquity, but the woman shall bear her iniquity.
>
> Numbers 5:27b, 31

Because wives were regarded in ancient Hebrew society as the sexual property of their husbands and not vice versa, no legal test of any form was provided for the woman who suspected that her husband had been unfaithful to her. As we have noted, even the very concept of a man commiting adultery against his wife was given no legal expression.

On the other hand, the unfaithful wife became a powerful symbol within Hebrew culture. Seven of the prophets described Israel as an unfaithful wife to God, and the Talmud (a large collection of rabbinical interpretations of the laws of Moses, assembled about A.D. 200) devoted a whole section to "the adulteress." However, no mention is made of the unfaithful husband.

Some have pointed out that Christians in our own age express this double standard by using the pronoun "she" when referring to the inferior and sinful church, stating that the church must entreat "her" Savior for mercy and grace. This language, they insist, implies that the feminine pronoun is a better vehicle than the masculine to express inferiority and guilt.

Seduction and rape as crimes against sexual property

The Mosaic laws regarding both seduction and rape bring the concept of women as sexual property into especially clear focus. A man who seduces a maiden, the law stated, must pay her father the amount normally given as a bride price for a virgin and then either marry her or not, depending entirely on the father's decision (Exodus 22:16–17).

A man who rapes a maiden, however (but only if the commission of his crime is witnessed!), shall pay the victim's father fifty shekels of silver and then marry her and never be allowed to divorce her (Deuteronomy 22:28–29). The woman herself is not given a choice over whether or not to marry her attacker.

In 2 Samuel 13 we find the sad story of the rape of Tamar, a daughter of King David, by one of her own brothers. In this account the rape victim herself was regarded as almost insignificant.

> David's son Absalom had a beautiful sister whose name was Tamar; and David's son Amnon fell in love with her. Amnon was so tormented that he made himself ill because of his sister Tamar, for she was a virgin and it seemed impossible to Amnon to do anything to her. But Amnon had a friend whose name was Jonadab, the son of David's brother Shimeah; and

Jonadab was a very crafty man. He said to him, "O son of the king, why are you so haggard morning after morning? Will you not tell me?" Amnon said to him, "I love Tamar, my brother Absalom's sister." Jonadab said to him, "Lie down on your bed, and pretend to be ill; and when your father comes to see you, say to him, 'Let my sister Tamar come and give me something to eat, and prepare the food in my sight, so that I may see it and eat it from her hand.'"

2 Samuel 13:1b–5

So Amnon took Jonadab's advice, pretending to be ill. When David came to visit his supposedly sick son, Amnon asked his father to have Tamar prepare him dinner.

Then David sent home to Tamar, saying, "Go to your brother Amnon's house, and prepare food for him." So Tamar went to her brother Amnon's house, where he was lying down. She took dough, kneaded it, made cakes in his sight, and baked the cakes. Then she took the pan and set them out before him, but he refused to eat. Amnon said, "Send out everyone from me." So everyone went out from him. Then Amnon said to Tamar, "Bring the food into the chamber, so that I may eat from your hand." So Tamar took the cakes she had made, and brought them into the chamber to Amnon her brother. But when she brought them near him to eat, he took hold of her, and said to her, "Come, lie with me, my sister." She answered him, "No, my brother, do not force me; for such a thing is not done in Israel; do not do anything so vile! As for me, where could I carry my shame? And as for you, you would be as one of the scoundrels in Israel. Now therefore, I beg you, speak to the king; for he will not withhold me from you." But he would not listen to her; and being stronger than she, he forced her and lay with her.

Then Amnon was seized with a very great loathing for her; indeed, his loathing was even greater than the lust he had felt for her. Amnon said to her, "Get out!" But she said to him, "No, my brother; for this wrong in sending me away is greater than the other that you did to me." But he would not listen to her. He called the young man who served him and said,

"Put this woman out of my presence, and bolt the door after her."

2 Samuel 13:7–17

Tamar put ashes on her head. She was clothed in a long robe with sleeves, the kind that only virgin daughters of the king wore. She tore this garment into shreds, put her hand on her head, and went away, crying aloud as she went.

> Her brother Absalom said to her, "Has Amnon your brother been with you? Be quiet for now, my sister; he is your brother; do not take this to heart." So Tamar remained, a desolate woman, in her brother Absalom's house.

2 Samuel 13:20

Tamar's voice still rises plaintively from the pages. Nonetheless, after reporting the crime in great detail, the storyteller then simply brushes Tamar aside. The subsequent narration is concerned only with the feelings of the men involved—Amnon, David, and Absalom—with no further attention given to Tamar. She is simply instructed to be quiet and not take the matter to heart!

Regarding women as sexual property tends to focus attention upon those men to whom the women belong. Even when the woman has been abused by a third party, as in the story of Tamar, the seriousness of such a crime is evaluated in terms of its effect, not upon the woman herself, but upon the men who perceive her as "theirs" (i.e., wife or daughter or sister) whom they must defend. So this story shifts from Tamar's plight to the question of what punishment her father and brother will extract from Amon for his sexual crime.

Incest and sexual property

Which sexual unions constitute incest? In our own culture, incest is generally based on genetic proximity. In the Old Testament, however, incest was defined according to the principle of sexual property. For that reason, we read of numerous marriages that in our own society would be forbidden. Nahor, for example, married his niece Milcah (Genesis 11:29), Abraham married his sister Sarah (Genesis 20:12), and Isaac married his cousin Rebekah (Genesis 24:15). No scandal was associated with Jacob's marriage to two of his cousins, Rachel and Leah (Genesis 29:12), or with Esau's marriage to his cousin Malhalath (Genesis 28:9), or with the union of Amram, Moses' father, to his own aunt (Numbers 26:59).

Notice that when Tamar was sexually accosted by her brother Amnon, she tried to talk him into marrying her instead of raping her. "The king," she insisted, referring to their father David, "will not withhold me from you" (2 Samuel 13:13). Her statement affirms that marriage between siblings (at least with paternal consent) was regarded as permissible in that society.[1]

Genesis 19:30–38 relates how Lot's two daughters got him drunk and then seduced him, in order to bear children of his lineage. This report does contain an implied criticism, in that the descendants of these two women became the ancestors of two of Israel's greatest enemy nations. However, the action on the part of Lot's daughters in and of itself received no censure, either from Lot or from God.

A change in incest laws

Eventually the kind of liaisons mentioned above came to be regarded as unlawful within ancient Israel. Strangely, they were forbidden by the Mosaic law for the same reason that they were acceptable to earlier generations—the belief that women are sexual property.

The following excerpt from the law of Moses (Leviticus 18:6–18) illustrates this (included in brackets are the names of those whose marriages would have been proscribed if the law had been in effect earlier, during the patriarchal period):

> None of you shall approach anyone near of kin to uncover nakedness: I am the LORD. You shall not uncover the nakedness of your father, which is the nakedness of your mother; she is your mother, you shall not uncover her nakedness. You shall not uncover the nakedness of your father's wife; it is the

nakedness of your father. You shall not uncover the nakedness of your sister, your father's daughter or your mother's
daughter, whether born at home or born abroad [violated by
Abraham]. You shall not uncover the nakedness of your son's
daughter or of your daughter's daughter, for their nakedness
is your own nakedness. You shall not uncover the nakedness
of your father's wife's daughter, begotten by your father, since
she is your sister. You shall not uncover the nakedness of your
father's sister; she is your father's flesh [violated by Amram].
You shall not uncover the nakedness of your mother's sister,
for she is your mother's flesh. You shall not uncover the nakedness of your father's brother, that is, you shall not approach his wife; she is your aunt. You shall not uncover the
nakedness of your daughter-in-law: she is your son's wife;
you shall not uncover her nakedness. You shall not uncover
the nakedness of your brother's wife; it is your brother's nakedness. You shall not uncover the nakedness of a woman
and her daughter, and you shall not take her son's daughter
or her daughter's daughter to uncover her nakedness; they
are your flesh; it is depravity. And you shall not take a woman
as a rival to her sister, uncovering her nakedness while her
sister is still alive [violated by Jacob].[2]

We have already noted that the practices that these laws
forbid are based on the concept of women as sexual property.
Surprisingly, these laws themselves are based on this very same
concept. To uncover a woman's nakedness, for example, is regarded in the law as uncovering her husband's nakedness. In
other words, a wife's own body belongs to her husband, so that
to misuse it is to trespass against his property.

Therefore, incest within Hebrew society was defined without any reference to genetics. It consisted of engaging in sexual
intercourse with the sexual property of one's father, one's paternal uncle, one's brother, or one's son, or—by extension—the
daughters of the wives of these relatives. Incest consisted of taking and using another man's sexual property.

During the patriarchal period, various marriages between
family members that once had been permitted with the father's

consent (after all, the woman involved was the father's property) centuries later became proscribed by the law of Moses (after all, the woman involved was the father's property).

To a certain degree incest is defined in modern western culture according to the concept of sexual proximity, if not sexual property. For example, in most states it is illegal for a person to marry his or her adopted sibling, even when they are not biologically related to each other. Although it may be lawful for a man to marry his stepmother, such a union would be regarded with disfavor in most communities.

Prostitution and sexual property

Because sexual moral codes were based on the concept of women as sexual property, prostitution in and of itself receives little if any condemnation in the Old Testament. We find no criticism leveled at Judah when he hired the sexual services of a prostitute (Genesis 38)—who was actually Tamar, his widowed daughter-in-law, in disguise (a different Tamar than the woman who was raped by Amnon). Moreover, Hosea stated that God will not punish prostitutes, since it was men of Israel who visited them (Hosea 4:12–14). In fact, Proverbs 6:23–29 declares quite openly that it is better to visit a prostitute than to commit adultery:

> For the commandment is a lamp and the teaching a light,
>   and the reproofs of discipline are the way of life,
> to preserve you from the wife of another,
>   from the smooth tongue of the adulteress.
> Do not desire her beauty in your heart,
>   and do not let her capture you with her eyelashes;
> for a prostitute's fee is only a loaf of bread,
>   but the wife of another stalks a man's very life.
> Can fire be carried in the bosom
>   without burning one's clothes?
> Or can one walk on hot coals
>   without scorching the feet?
> So is he who sleeps with his neighbor's wife;
>   no one who touches her will go unpunished.

Ironically, those who favor the legalization of prostitution in our own culture often argue from the opposite point of view, stating that we own our own bodies and therefore have the right to sell sexual pleasures.

Women who used sex as a weapon

The notion that women are sexual property provides a background to two stories of women who used their sexual charms to control powerful men.

The first concerns a Persian king named Ahasuerus, who, in a drunken condition during a royal banquet, orders his beautiful wife, Vashti, to display herself before his guests. She refuses to do so, causing the king to become angry. He asks his advisors what he should do with Vashti. They express the fear that her behavior will become an example for other women. If that happens, the king is told, then wives might "look with contempt upon their husbands" (Esther 1:17). The result, the advisors predict, "will be no end of contempt and wrath" (Esther 1:18).[3] So the king deposes Vashti from her position as queen. He then initiates a search for a replacement.

Esther, described as "fair and beautiful" (2:7), wins the king's favor and performs her duties as the new queen. Later, when a pogrom is initiated against the Jews, Esther uses her feminine loveliness to wield political influence. She manages to sway the king's judgment and thereby rescue her people from destruction.

The second story, found in the Apocrypha, centers on a stunningly beautiful widow named Judith. She too uses her sexual attractiveness to save her people.

Judith's city is under siege from the Assyrian army, led by a general named Holofernes. She prays to God this earnest petition: "By the deceit of my lips strike down the slave with the prince;...crush their arrogance by the hand of a woman" (Judith 9:10).

Judith then instills in Holofernes a great desire to possess her. Eventually she gains an invitation into his tent, gets him drunk, and assassinates him in his bed. Judith then summarizes her success by stating, "it was my face that seduced him to his destruction" (13:16).

In each of these two stories a beautiful woman uses the desire of a man to possess her in order to achieve her purpose. In each case the purpose is altruistic (although Holofernes might have some personal misgivings about that statement!). Nonetheless, these stories suggest that in a society where women are regarded as sexual property, men may place too much value on physical beauty and underestimate the willingness of women to utilize their sexual attractiveness for their own agenda.

The concept of women as sexual property, to be used and protected by men, shaped Mosaic laws and determined the relationship of husbands and wives, from the lowliest Hebrew home to the royal palace itself.

Both Jesus and Paul rejected (see Chapters 6 and 7) this concept as unjust for women and at variance with God's original design for human marriages (see Chapter 5). Unfortunately the church, early in its history, affirmed the cultural principle of sexual property and perpetuated its practice with only slight modification.

Notes

[1] There were laws prohibiting the marrying of close relatives (Leviticus 18:6–18; 20:11–12; Deuteronomy 27:20, 22–23); however, these laws would have forbidden the marital examples just named as well as the practice of levirate marriages (see next chapter). Moreover, since these laws were based on the principle of women as sexual property, it is possible that they could be set aside if the woman's father agreed.

[2] Cf Deuteronomy 27:20, 22–23 and Leviticus 20:11–12.

[3] Cf Sirach 25:25–26:
"Allow no outlet to water,
        and no boldness of speech to an evil wife.
If she does not go as you direct,
        separate her from yourself."

Questions for Discussion

1. Are there any identifiable groups in our own culture that tend to regard women as sexual possessions?

2. Does using the terms *baby* and *mine* in referring to one's lover reveal a sense of sexual possessiveness?

3. To what extent is the sexual double standard still operative in our own society?

4. In ancient Israel there was a close association between the king's concubines and the king's authority. In what ways, if any, are sexuality and power linked today?

5. Is there a moral difference between having an extramarital affair and engaging the sexual services of a prostitute?

6. Several years ago a Christian writer described sexual intercourse as a sacrament. In what ways, if any, would you agree with that statement? Disagree?

2

Did the Devil Invent Sex While God Was Napping?

Even today some Christians imply that sexuality was invented by the Devil while God's back was turned. As a person once observed, "there is something about sexuality that blows the ecclesiastical mind."

Early in the church's history many Christians were convinced that sexual intimacy was an evil snare unto damnation. They regarded celibacy as a mark of superior spirituality, to the point that some sincerely believed that only virgins would be admitted into heaven.

The Bible itself, however, begins with the contrasting viewpoint, that sexuality is a blessing and sexual intimacy is a gracious part of God's design. According to the author of Genesis, we are sexual beings precisely because God designed us that way. It is God who intentionally made us male and female. Our sexuality is one aspect of the creative design that God described as "very good" (Genesis 1:31). Sexuality—and the mutual pleasure derived from it—is a gift from God, a precious part of his handiwork.

This appreciation for God's design is echoed in the Song of Solomon, a mildly erotic biblical writing that glorifies love and applauds the sensual delight one may receive from his or her partner's body.

In addition to being a source of mutual pleasure, sexual intercourse was regarded in Hebrew society as the sign and seal of a marriage contract.

> But in the evening he [Laban] took his daughter Leah and brought her to Jacob; and he [Jacob] went in to her.
>
> Genesis 29:23

> So Jacob went in to Rachel also, and he loved Rachel more than Leah.
>
> Genesis 29:30a

In contrast to the later negative attitudes about sex held by some Jewish aesthetes, Stoic philosophers, and church fathers, the Old Testament openly celebrates sex as a gift of the Creator, a seal of the marriage covenant and a delight to lovers.

Sex as worship

On the other hand, the concept that sexual intercourse may be regarded as an act of worship receives severe and repeated censure throughout the Old Testament.[1] The extensive number of references to cultic prostitution indicates that it was an incessant problem in Hebrew society.

Selling sexual pleasure on behalf of a temple or a pagan deity was a widespread practice in the ancient Near East, one that was quite old by the time of Abraham. Sumerian inscriptions at the end of the fourth millennium before Christ tell of rituals designed to re-enact the sacred marriage of Inanna (goddess of the storehouse) to Dumuzi (god of the date palm). Their marriage was regarded as "the sacred cosmic sexual act in which all nature is fertilized."[2]

In a similar manner the Canaanites celebrated the sexual union of the god Yarih and moon goddess Nikkal. According to the mythic poetry, Yarith says: "I shall make her field into a vineyard/The field of her love into an orchard."[3]

Hebrew prophets often warned their countrymen against worshiping Asherah, a fertility goddess whose symbols were a tree and the female pubic triangle.[4]

The worship of fertility goddesses, such as Asherah, Artemis, Aphrodite, and Cybele, often involved sexual intercourse. This practice was a form of sympathetic magic, wherein an action is performed with the intention of enlisting the unseen spirit world into performing a similar, broader action. (Compare the ancient ritual of sticking a pin into a doll as a magical attempt to make a particular person experience pain or illness.) Sexual intercourse during worship served as a magical appeal for divine empowerment in the fertility of crops, livestock, and humans.

The role of sacred prostitute was maintained throughout most of ancient history in eastern Mediterranean cultures. For example, in Babylon three classes of prostitutes were associated with the worship of the goddess Ishtar. A Greek traveler named Herodotus wrote that the temple of Aphrodite in Corinth boasted the deployment of a thousand prostitutes.

Sacred prostitutes were usually female, and few of them lived to see their thirtieth birthdays. Some sacred prostitutes, however, were male. Three Old Testament passages refer to male prostitutes in Israel during the reigns of Rehoboam and Asa:

> ...there were also male temple prostitutes in the land. They committed all the abominations of the nations that the LORD drove out before the people of Israel.
>
> 1 Kings 14:24

He put away the male temple prostitutes out of the land, and removed all the idols that his ancestors had made.

1 Kings 15:12

The remnant of the male temple prostitutes who were still in the land in the days of his father Asa, he exterminated.

1 Kings 22:46

Hebrew rejection of fertility cults was not a rejection of sex

As we have already noted, these sex/magic practices were grounded in ancient myths that described creation as resulting from the copulation of deities. Unlike their neighboring cultures, however, the Hebrews believed that the world and its rich varieties of life came into being, not from the impregnation of goddesses, but from the creative power of God's spoken word (Genesis 1:3, etc.). So the Israelites and their neighbors differed not only in their theological speculation about the origin of the world, but also in their opposing convictions about the relationship of sexual union and worship.

Nonetheless, the objections against cultic prostitution, raised by Hebrew prophets and lawmakers alike, failed to eradicate its practice in ancient Israel. The very existence of laws forbidding this activity indicates that cultic prostitution was regarded as a serious and pernicious threat to Israel's faith. The Hebrew scriptures report that both male and female sacred prostitutes were associated with even the temple in Jerusalem.

The practice of sacred prostitution was challenged by King Josiah, who initiated a bloody religious reform against the worship of a variety of pagan deities in "high places" (on hilltops under sacred trees or poles) and in the temple itself:

The king commanded the high priest Hilkiah, the priests of the second order, and the guardians of the threshold, to bring out of the temple of the LORD all the vessels made for Baal, for Asherah, and for all the host of heaven; he burned them outside Jerusalem in the fields of the Kidron, and carried their ashes to Bethel. He deposed the idolatrous priests whom the kings of Judah had ordained to make offerings in the high places at the cities of Judah and around Jerusalem; those also who made offerings to Baal, to the sun, the moon, the constellations, and all the host of the heavens. He brought out the image of Asherah from the house of the LORD, outside Jerusalem, to the Wadi Kidron, burned it at the Wadi Kidron, beat it to dust and threw the dust of it upon the graves of the common people. He broke down the houses of the male temple prostitutes that were in the house of the LORD, where the women did weaving for Asherah. He brought all the priests out of the towns of Judah, and defiled the high places where the priests had made offerings, from Geba to Beer-sheba; he broke down the high places of the gates that were at the entrance of the gate of Joshua the governor of the city, which were on the left at the gate of the city.

2 Kings 23:4–8

Josiah's purge then extended beyond Jerusalem.

He broke the pillars in pieces, cut down the sacred poles, and covered the sites with human bones.

Moreover, the altar at Bethel, the high place erected by Jeroboam son of Nebat, who caused Israel to sin—he pulled down that altar along with the high place. He burned the high place, crushing it to dust; he also burned the sacred pole....Moreover, Josiah removed all the shrines of the high places that were in the towns of Samaria, which kings of Israel had made, provoking the LORD to anger; he did to them just as he had done at Bethel. He slaughtered on the altars all the priests of the high places who were there, and burned human bones on them. Then he returned to Jerusalem.

2 Kings 23:14–15,19–20

Archaeologists have discovered hundreds of zoological and human figurines near the location of the temple in Jerusalem, all of them broken, indicating that they may have been used in the worship of Baal and Asherah until they were removed and destroyed during King Josiah's reform.

Cultic prostitution was so widespread and well known during biblical times that it became a symbol for religious apostasy among both Hebrew prophets and New Testament writers. Turning away from God was described as adultery or fornication, and the word image of Israel going after foreign whores was meant to be regarded both figuratively and literally. In the New Testament this same imagery was used to refer to those who would in turn abandon their faith in Christ. In Revelation 2:18–23 we read of the risen Christ saying to one congregation:

> And to the angel of the church in Thyatira write: These are the words of the Son of God, who has eyes like a flame of fire, and whose feet are like burnished bronze: I know your works—your love, faith, service, and patient endurance. I know that your last works are greater than the first. But I have this against you: you tolerate that woman Jezebel, who calls herself a prophet and is teaching and beguiling my servants to practice fornication and to eat food sacrificed to idols. I gave her time to repent, but she refuses to repent of her fornication. Beware, I am throwing her on a bed, and those who commit adultery with her I am throwing into great distress, unless they repent of her doings; and I will strike her children dead. And all the churches will know that I am the one who searches minds and hearts, and I will give to each of you as your works deserve.

This concept of sex as a means of worshiping divine sources of fertility provides a background for the frequent biblical injunction against the worship of a goddess. Readers today sometimes assume that these warnings reflect an inherently male bias; the issue, however, was much more complex than that. As British scholar Mary Hayter reminds us, "To suggest antipathy to the Goddess was the result of some inherently male-chauvinist aspect of Hebrew thought simply trivializes the whole subject."[5]

When the Hebrew scriptures became read and known throughout the Mediterranean world as part of the church's collection of sacred writings, many persons assumed that those passages that forbade sacred prostitution also forbade sexual intimacy of any kind.

Moreover, in the book of Revelation (the last to be included in the Christian canon) special attention is given to 144,000 men who stand with the Lamb in Zion and who have the name of the Savior and his Father's name written on their foreheads. These men are those "who have not defiled themselves with women, for they are virgins" (Revelation 14:4).

Therefore, although the Bible opens with a sense that sexuality is a part of God's "very good" creation, it closes with a suggestion that only those who are virgins will enter the new heaven.

The denigration of sex in the Greco-Roman world

As was mentioned earlier, many leaders within the early church tended to regard sexual intimacy as intrinsically unholy and wrong—an attitude that persisted down through the centuries. The origin of this disdain toward sexual pleasures was not simply their understanding of the scriptures. This attitude found its roots deep within the philosophy of the Hellenic world.

As the church expanded into the Gentile world, converts brought with them the philosophical perspectives of their own culture, by which they interpreted the scriptures.

The most popular school of thought in Greco-Roman society was that of Stoicism, which tended to regard sexual appetite and marriage with disfavor.[6] Accompanying this was a fairly widespread attitude that regarded the human body as inherently evil, to be subdued by the mind through disciplined philosophical training, or by the spirit through mystic experience. Therefore certain Gnostic writers taught that the original sin of Adam and Eve was sexual intercourse (a notion that prompted St. Augustine to exclaim, *"Illud est ridiculum!"*).

Many stoic philosophers regarded women as a serious distraction to those men who would otherwise choose the higher pursuit of knowledge. Pliny the Younger (AD 61–113), for example, argued that sexual intercourse even in marriage was acceptable only if its purpose was to produce children.

In addition, the conviction of Aristotle that women were inferior to men was soon reflected in the literature and preaching of the early church.

In like manner many Jewish rabbis warned young men that women would distract them from the higher pursuit of wisdom. Members of the Jewish party known as Essenes (a portion of whom lived at Qumran and produced the Dead Sea Scrolls) were expected to marry and sire children, then leave their wives and await the coming of God's intervention in history.

The denigration of sex in the early church

The heretical Marcion (who died about the year 154) regarded marriage as "filthiness" and "obscene." His disciples called the human body a "nest of guilt." This attitude was shared by numerous orthodox church leaders as well.

Many such leaders went so far as to preach the doctrine of *encratism*, the belief that only virgins will be granted salvation. Tatian, for example, who was a pupil of Justin Martyr (about 100–165), traveled east from Rome preaching the message that chastity and vegetarianism were required for salvation. Several years before that, the bishop of Cnossos referred to the teaching that not all Christians need be celibate as "slop" instead of nourishment.

A variety of writings, spuriously attributed to apostolic authorship or else purporting to relate actual events in the lives of apostles, extolled the virtues of celibacy. One such spurious document, *Paul and Thecla*, written by a presbyter in Asia Minor during the late second century, claimed that the apostle Paul made the doctrine of encratism a central tenet of his evangelistic message.

Another such late second century writing depicted the apostle Andrew informing an aristocratic woman that marriage was "foul and polluted" and arguing that only by forswearing sex could a person nullify the sin of Adam. Another such writing related how Jesus appeared in a couple's bridal chamber and told them that their marriage should never be consummated because sex was dirty.

Meanwhile, Tertullian (about 160–230) argued against marriage for Christians. At one point he tried to persuade Christian men to be satisfied with "spiritual marriages," urging each man to marry several widows who are "fair in faith, dowered with poverty, sealed with age." Tertullian distinguished marriage and fornication only in terms of legitimacy.

Cyprian, bishop of Carthage, remarked that a certain plague was of some benefit in that it allowed Christian virgins to die unspoiled. Athenagoras, while defending the faith, remarked that "of course virginity brings a man closer to God." The repugnance toward sex among these early pagan converts to Christianity reached such a proportion that, for a while at least, the idea was entertained in Syriac churches of withholding baptism from any males who would not take a vow of celibacy.

Clement of Alexandria (about 150–220) found it necessary to argue heatedly against influential persons who taught that marriage was nothing more than arranged prostitution.

When Augustine (354–430), who had lived a life of sexual excesses, became a Christian, he also became celibate. (Apparently the idea that one could be both a Christian and a husband/father never entered his mind.) Augustine regarded marriage as "a covenant with death." He stated that sexual desire "is only to be tolerated in marriage. It is not a good which comes out of the essence of marriage, but an evil which is the accident of original sin." To actually enjoy sexual intercourse, he argued, makes "the bridal chamber a brothel."

Although the doctrine of encratism was not accepted by the church as a whole, a belief that Mary remained a virgin all of her life gained wide acceptance, thereby increasing the respect among Christians toward those who remained celibate. Jerome (340?–420), famous for his translation of the Hebrew Old Testament and Greek New Testament into Latin, persuasively extolled the spiritual benefits of virginity. Jerome borrowed a scale from Jesus' parable of the seeds and rated virginity at 100, widow-hood at 60, and marriage at 30. Jerome once wrote a work entitled *Against Jovian*, in which he opposed a certain monk on the question of celibacy. Jovian had given up the celibate life, reasoning that all persons—celibate and married—are equal before God. Jerome was surprised at the negative public response his writing received.

Gregory of Nyssa, a contemporary of Jerome, taught that if Adam and Eve had not sinned, then reproduction among humans would be accomplished by some means other than sexual intercourse. This belief was shared by others, including the most influential of theologians, Thomas Aquinas (1225?–1274).

As a result of this widespread debate over the question of the rightness or wrongness of sexual intimacy, the church made two important, mutually contradictory, decisions. Marriage came to be elevated to the status of a sacrament; however, the church's priests (in the West, at least) were required to forego this sacrament and remain celibate.

These conflicting attitudes toward sexual intimacy are reflected in different teachings and practices among churches today. The Roman Catholic church continues to regard procreation as the sole purpose of sexual intimacy and to demand that all its priests and nuns remain celibate (except those priests who were already married when they converted to Catholicism).

Many Protestant churches, on the other hand, are very reluctant to hire unmarried ministers, fearing that a pastor who is not married cannot empathize and counsel those who are. Such churches also tend to offer a warmer welcome to married couples than to single adults and to provide programs designed more for families than for singles.

Orthodox priests are allowed to marry, but the names of those who do choose marriage are usually passed over whenever candidates are selected for the office of bishop.

Moreover, in spite of the open frankness of the scriptures regarding sex and in spite of the importance of that subject for individuals and society, relatively few churches of any branch of

Christianity offer educational courses on human sexuality and sexual ethics.

All of these facts support the argument that the church as a whole still carries within its collective psyche the ambivalence regarding sexual pleasure that characterized Hellenistic thought and culture. To put it bluntly, when it comes to sexual matters, the attitudes found in most churches are far more pagan than biblical.

Notes

[1]The one Old Testament general law against prostitution (Leviticus 19:29) was probably aimed at this religious practice. A more specific law states that if a priest's daughter becomes a cultic prostitute, he is profaned and she is to be burned to death (Leviticus 21:9).

[2]Thorkild Jacobson, *The Treasures of Darkness* (New Haven: Yale U. Press, 1976), p. 47.

[3]Cyrus Gordon, *Ugarit and Minoan Crete* (New York: Norton, 1966), p. 99.

[4]See "Understanding Asherah," by Ruth Hestrin, *Biblical Archaeology Review*, xvii, 5 (Sept/Oct 1991), p. 50.

[5]Mary Hayter, *The New Eve in Christ* (Grand Rapids: Eerdmans, 1987), p. 17.

[6]For example, Epictitus, *Discourses* 3.7 § 19–22; Sonorus, *Gynaec.* 1.28–33.

Questions for Discussion

1. Are there any ways that sexual attraction is associated with worship today?

2. What persons or groups today are most influential in shaping our society's attitudes regarding sexual intimacy?

3. To what extent has our society inherited the Hebrew idea that sexuality is "very good"?

4. To what extent has our society inherited the notion that sexuality is a hindrance to our intellectual and/or spiritual development? Is this problem modified by the lessening of social mores regarding sexual intercourse between unmarried adults?

5. In this chapter the claim is made that churches perpetuate contradictory messages regarding sexual intimacy. Do you agree? Do you see other ways that this is evident? What changes would you recommend?

3

Why Biblical People
Did Not Marry for Love

In our own society, the choice
of a marriage partner rests almost solely upon the mutual decision of the couple themselves. The man and woman become
acquainted with each other and determine their suitability during dating. Their final decision regarding marriage usually depends heavily upon their feelings—whether or not they decide
they love each other enough to make a commitment.

The peoples of the Bible chose marriage partners in quite a
different manner. The selection was seldom left up to the couple
alone. Many times the couple did not have an opportunity to
meet until only briefly before their wedding. Love was viewed
as a delightful passion, a priceless emotional gift.

Set me as a seal upon your heart,
　　as a seal upon your arm;
for love is strong as death,
　　passion fierce as the grave.
Its flashes are flashes of fire,
　　a raging flame.
Many waters cannot quench love,
　　neither can floods drown it.
If one offered for love
　　all the wealth of his house,
　　it would be utterly scorned.

　　　　　　　　　　　　　　Song of Solomon 8:6–7

Yet as desirable as love might be, nonetheless it was regarded in biblical times as something that arose during marriage, not as a necessary prelude to it.

Arranged marriages

We do not know how a brother and sister named Abraham and Sarah came to be married to each other. However, we are told what happened when Abraham decided it was time for their son Isaac to be married. (After all, Isaac was only forty years old at the time, hardly mature enough to make such an important choice for himself!)

The story of Isaac and Rebekah provides an entertaining illustration of how marriages were arranged in the ancient Near East.

Abraham took aside his most trusted servant and requested that he swear to fulfill Abraham's instructions exactly (Genesis 24:1–11). The servant make his oath while holding onto Abraham's testicles—a symbolic act by which he was agreeing to be responsible even to Abraham's descendants. (Incidentally, in this ancient ritual of oath-taking we find the origin of the English word *testify*.)

Abraham sent this servant all the way to Abraham's homeland—from Israel across the Fertile Crescent into what is present-day Iraq—in order to select a wife for Isaac from among Abraham's kindred.

Upon arriving, the servant first narrowed down the selection to a woman who was related to Abraham, who was young, who was attractive, and who was hospitable to strangers. Having established these standards, he left the final choice of the specific woman up to God.

> He made the camels kneel down outside the city by the well of water; it was toward evening, the time when women go out to draw water. And he said, "O LORD, God of my master Abraham, please grant me success today and show steadfast love to my master Abraham. I am standing here by the spring of water, and the daughters of the townspeople are coming out to draw water. Let the girl to whom I shall say, 'Please offer your jar that I may drink,' and who shall say, 'Drink, and I will water your camels'— let her be the one whom you have appointed for your servant Isaac. By this I shall know that you have shown steadfast love to my master."
>
> Before he had finished speaking, there was Rebekah, who was born to Bethuel son of Milcah, the wife of Nahor, Abraham's brother, coming out with her water jar on her shoulder. The girl was very fair to look upon, a virgin, whom no man had known. She went down to the spring, filled her jar, and came up. Then the servant ran to meet her and said, "Please let me sip a little water from your jar." "Drink, my lord," she said, and quickly lowered her jar upon her hand and gave him a drink. When she had finished giving him a drink, she said, "I will draw for your camels also, until they have finished drinking." So she quickly emptied her jar into the trough and ran again to the well to draw, and she drew for all his camels.
>
> Genesis 24:11–20

Then, after noting that this young woman met and exceeded all of the details of his petition, the servant then wondered to himself if possibly his prayer had been answered (verse 21)!

The story continues, embodying the essential requirements in arranging a marriage. Abraham's servant negotiated with

Rebekah's two guardians, her father Bethuel and her brother Laban. He told them of Isaac's background, how he was the son of their relative Abraham—who, the servant assured them, had much wealth. Then the servant related to them how Abraham commissioned him to secure for Isaac a wife from among his kinsmen, and how a prayer had led him to Rebekah.

> Then Laban and Bethuel answered, "The thing comes from the LORD; we cannot speak to you anything bad or good. Look, Rebekah is before you, take her and go, and let her be the wife of your master's son, as the LORD has spoken."
>
> When Abraham's servant heard their words, he bowed himself to the ground before the LORD.
>
> Genesis 24:50–52

At this point the negotiations were almost complete. All that remained was for Abraham's servant to present a bride-price to Rebekah's family and for them to secure her formal acceptance of the contract and then give her a dowry. The bride-price is identified in verse 53:

> And the servant brought out jewelry of silver and of gold, and garments, and gave them to Rebekah; he also gave to her brother and to her mother costly ornaments.

Bethuel and Laban offered extended hospitality to Abraham's servant, but he expressed his wish to return quickly to his master. So the men secured Rebekah's acceptance and presented her with a dowry in the form of female servants. Then they offered Rebekah their blessing.

> They said, "We will call the girl, and ask her." And they called Rebekah, and said to her, "Will you go with this man?" She said, "I will." So they sent away their sister Rebekah and her nurse along with Abraham's servant and his men. And they blessed Rebekah and said to her,
>   "May you, our sister, become
>   thousands of myriads;
>   may your offspring gain possession
>   of the gates of their foes."

> Then Rebekah and her maids rose up, mounted the camels, and followed the man; thus the servant took Rebekah, and went his way.
>
> Genesis 24:57–61

Rebekah was accompanied by her nurse (whom, we may assume, Rebekah had known all of her life) as well as by several of her maids. In our culture today, a bride and groom set up housekeeping by themselves, thereby depending heavily upon each other for companionship and friendship. Rebekah, however, did not enter into marriage alone. She took with her into her new home several familiar faces, persons whom she valued and trusted.

Also unlike modern marriages, Rebekah and Isaac met each other only after the contract was established. They sealed their marriage covenant with sexual intercourse, and (as with all good marriages in biblical times) they gradually fell in love.

> Isaac went out in the evening to walk in the field; and looking up, he saw camels coming. And Rebekah looked up, and when she saw Isaac, she slipped quickly from the camel, and said to the servant, "Who is the man over there, walking in the field to meet us?" The servant said, "It is my master." So she took her veil and covered herself. And the servant told Isaac all the things that he had done. Then Isaac brought her into his mother Sarah's tent. He took Rebekah, and she became his wife; and he loved her. So Isaac was comforted after his mother's death.
>
> Genesis 24:63–67

Isaac's marriage was arranged according his father's instructions. One of Isaac's sons, however, made his own marital choices. He selected the kind of women he knew his father would not want him to marry.

Isaac had twin sons, Esau and Jacob. According to the patriarchal system, the firstborn of the two, Esau, should eventually receive their father's blessing—a ritual that invested the eldest son with ultimate authority and responsibility over the whole family (including his brother).

However, Jacob managed to impersonate Esau and thereby receive the blessing for himself, a deceit that Isaac honored. Esau was furious at his loss. Having heard Isaac instruct Jacob not to marry a Canaanite woman from the region in which they lived, Esau proceeded to do just that. He selected the kind of wife who would most upset his father. He married out of revenge.

> Now Esau saw that Isaac had blessed Jacob and sent him away to Paddan-aram to take a wife from there, and that as he blessed him he charged him, "You shall not marry one of the Canaanite women," and that Jacob had obeyed his father and his mother and gone to Paddan-aram. So when Esau saw that the Canaanite women did not please his father Isaac, Esau went to Ishmael and took Mahalath daughter of Abraham's son Ishmael, and sister of Nebaioth, to be his wife in addition to the wives he had.
>
> Genesis 28:6–9

Choosing a wife based on sex appeal

There were a number of criteria (other than revenge) for selecting marriage partners among the fascinating peoples of the Bible. Basing the choice of a marriage partner on sexual attractiveness, however, was usually represented in the stories of the Bible as a prelude to disaster.

For example, King David chose Bathsheba because of her sex appeal (amply displayed as she was taking a bath at a location that could be viewed from the royal palace). His sexual covetousness indirectly led David to arrange to have Bathsheba's husband killed in battle (2 Samuel 11).

A brief story earlier in the Bible (Genesis 34:1–26) tells of an incident involving rape, duplicity, greed, and war among nomadic desert dwellers. It also presents love and sexual attraction as inadequate reasons for marriage.

One day a local prince named Shechem saw Jacob's daughter Dinah traveling to visit with some of the women of that region. Shechem seized Dinah and raped her. Afterwards he spoke tenderly to his victim and swore that he loved her. Then this young prince went to his father, Hamor, and demanded, "Get me this girl to be my wife."

Instead of disciplining his son for his crime, Hamor acquiesced to his son's entreaties and took Shechem with him to Jacob's tent. Making no mention of the violent behavior of his son, Hamor began marriage negotiations with Jacob. "The heart of my son Shechem longs for your daughter," Hamor began. "Please give her to him in marriage."

Jacob, already aware of the crime of Shechem, said nothing. He was waiting for his strong sons to return from tending to their cattle. They arrived soon after Hamor began his appeal.

The old man looked at the stern faces of Jacob's offspring. "Make marriages with us; give your daughters to us, and take our daughters for yourselves," Hamor urged. Then he pointed out to them the economic advantages of such marital unions: "You shall live with us; and the land shall be open to you; live and trade in it, and get property in it."

Shechem then entered into the negotiations. "Let me find favor with you, and whatever you say to me I will give," he promised Jacob. "Put the marriage present and gift as high as you like, and I will give whatever you ask me; only give me the girl to be my wife."

Jacob's sons withdrew and carefully crafted their response. "We cannot...give our sister to one who is uncircumcised, for that would be a disgrace to us," they declared. "Only on this condition will we consent to you: that you will become as we are and every male among you be circumcised." Then they would give their own daughters in marriage to Hamor's clansmen and marry their women in return. Turning to Shechem, they stated firmly, "But if you will not listen to us and be circumcised, then we will take [Dinah] and be gone."

Hamor returned to his own people and passionately persuaded the men to be circumcised, virtually promising them all of Jacob's wealth in return. The males agreed and underwent the painful process of circumcision.

While the men were recovering, however, two of Jacob's sons, Simeon and Levi, snuck into the city and killed all of the males, including Hamor and Shechem. They rescued Dinah and migrated on to another region.

The marriage of Shechem and Dinah has several similarities with that of Isaac and Rebekah. Abraham—through an agent—negotiated on behalf of his son, Isaac. Hamor negotiated on behalf of his son, Shechem. Moreover, in both cases a bride-price was involved, and the wealth of the groom's family was openly discussed.

The difference between the two accounts was Shechem's motivation. His desire to marry Dinah was fueled by uncontrolled sexual passion and romantic love. Whatever amount of love he professed to have for Dinah could not atone for his sexual attack upon her, at least not in the eyes of her brothers (the storyteller does not inform us of Dinah's feelings in this matter). So her brothers pretend to agree to the union, with one requirement—a provision that left Shechem and his male relatives unable to engage in sexual intercourse or to defend themselves in battle.

From the storyteller's perspective, the threefold elements of love, sexual attraction, and wealth do not constitute an adequate basis for marriage. Contrary to marriage customs in modern western societies, a fourth element was essential among biblical peoples: the families of both parties must agree to the marital union.

The right use of sexual attraction

A semi-erotic love poem in the Bible called the Song of Solomon (also known as the Song of Songs) celebrates sexual pleasure within marriage, but it does not present sex appeal as the basis for choosing a mate. For example, we read (8:8):

> We have a little sister,
>   and she has no breasts.
> What shall we do for our sister,
>   on the day when she is spoken for?

Notice that the problem is not that their little sister will remain unmarried. The fear is that her husband might not find her sexually stimulating *after* they are married.

Our own culture places a great emphasis on the role of sexual attraction in choosing a marriage partner. The biblical perspective challenges our society in this matter. Basing one's choice of a marriage partner primarily upon sex appeal, the biblical stories seem to say, is likely to foster unhappiness and perhaps even violence.

Instead of regarding sexual attraction as a prelude to marriage, as we do in contemporary society, the Song of Solomon passage reflects a quite different perspective. Sexual attraction is to be cultivated, not as a prelude to marriage, but as an essential and delightful part of the marriage itself.

Choosing a husband for his money

Both David and his son and successor Solomon chose wives on the basis of economic and political advantages. They married the daughters of other kings, those who ruled neighboring nations, in order to demonstrate good faith in establishing peace treaties and trade agreements.

Solomon managed to secure quite a number of these marriage alliances. We read in 1 Kings 11:3 concerning Solomon: "Among his wives were seven hundred princesses and three hundred concubines; and his wives turned away his heart [from God]."

People in the Bible often chose their marriage partners on the basis of economic security. The charming story of Ruth, for example, tells how this poor young widow enticed Boaz, a rich relative of her deceased husband, into marrying her. At the advice of her late husband's mother, Ruth sought out Boaz and slept with him. She did so because he was "a prominent rich man" (2:1) and he could offer her financial security (3:1). She did not pursue him for his looks or his wisdom. It was his house and barn she was after!

Economics were the basis also of the strange custom of levirate marriage, in which a man must marry his widowed sister-in-law if the man's brother had died without siring any sons.

The practice of levirate marriages was not limited to Hebrew society. Assyrian laws provided for the same kind of arrangement. For example, Law 33 from the Middle Assyrian Tablet A specifies that if a woman is widowed and has no sons "her father-in-law shall marry her to the son of his choice...."

The law regarding this form of matrimony is found in Deuteronomy 25:5–10:

> When brothers reside together, and one of them dies and has no son, the wife of the deceased shall not be married outside the family to a stranger. Her husband's brother shall go in to her, taking her in marriage, and performing the duty of a husband's brother to her, and the firstborn whom she bears shall succeed to the name of the deceased brother, so that his name may not be blotted out of Israel. But if the man has no desire to marry his brother's widow, then his brother's widow shall go up to the elders at the gate and say, "My husband's brother refuses to perpetuate his brother's name in Israel; he will not perform the duty of a husband's brother to me." Then the elders of his town shall summon him and speak to him. If he persists, saying, "I have no desire to marry her," then his brother's wife shall go up to him in the presence of the elders, pull his sandal off his foot, spit in his face, and declare, "This is what is done to the man who does not build up his brother's house." Throughout Israel his family shall be known as "the house of him whose sandal was pulled off."

The purpose of this law was not simply to insure support for a widow—although it did just that for widows in certain circumstances. The law's primary purpose, however, was to preserve the ownership of property within a family by providing a male heir. This practice of levirate was regarded as so important to the family's economic interest that a man who refused to marry his widowed sister-in-law became a disgrace to his whole clan.

Genesis 38 tells a fascinating story of how one woman disguised herself as a prostitute in order to provide a substitute for levirate marriage. The account begins with the death of Judah's firstborn son, Er, who was survived by his wife, Tamar (not the Tamar, daughter of King David, who was raped by her brother). As eldest son, Er would have become the new patriarch of the family after Judah's death and would have inherited the wealth and power that came with this position.

Acting according to the principle of levirate marriage, Judah ordered his second son, Onan, to marry Tamar in order to produce offspring, an heir for Er's estate. Onan, however, wanting to inherit all his deceased brother would have received, practiced *coitus interruptus,* purposefully withdrawing before ejaculation in the hope of not impregnating Tamar. However, Onan too died. Judah delayed in ordering his youngest son, Shelah, to marry Tamar. Judah was afraid that Shelah too might die, so he sent Tamar back to her father's house. Tamar had the law on her side, but Judah simply put her off and told her to wait until Shelah was older.

Tamar, however, was also growing older. So she devised a bold scheme. She disguised herself as a prostitute and sold her services to Judah himself, becoming pregnant by him. This way Tamar provided an heir to her deceased husband's share of the family estate and gained considerable economic advantage for herself.

Judah, upon being informed of Tamar's deceit, simply said, "She is more in the right than I, since I did not give her to my son Shelah" (Genesis 38:26).

The grudging respect that Judah had for his audacious daughter-in-law typifies the biblical attitude toward marriage for economic advantage. Both Ruth and Tamar are presented as resourceful and praiseworthy.

The marriages of Solomon, however, are remembered as having been made for economic reasons alone, without consideration of religious beliefs and practices. That kind of marriage is presented as a grievous mistake.

Marrying for love

Love is celebrated in the scriptures, especially in the Song of Solomon (or Song of Songs, as it is sometimes called), where we read (8:6–7):

> Set me as a seal upon your heart,
>   as a seal upon your arm;
> for love is strong as death,
>   passion fierce as the grave.
> Its flashes are flashes of fire,
>   a raging flame.
> Many waters cannot quench love,
>   neither can floods drown it.
> If one offered for love
>   all the wealth of his house,
>   it would be utterly scorned.

In spite of this high tribute to love, the idea of "falling in love and getting married" is rather recent. The only example found in the Bible of a person marrying for love is that of Jacob. Noticing how Rachel was "graceful and beautiful," he offered her father Laban seven years of labor for Rachel in lieu of the bride price. His only motive for marrying Rachel, we read, was that he loved her (Genesis 29:18), so much so that the seven years of labor "seemed to him but a few days because of the love he had for her" (verse 20).

However, his love for Rachel was also his reason for marrying her sister Leah! Laban switched daughters in the dark after the wedding ceremony. The next morning, when Jacob found Leah rather than Rachel in the bridal chamber with him, he stormed out and confronted his new father-in-law. Laban shrugged his shoulders and gave Jacob a "how can I help it?" look, claiming that it was not right to marry off a younger daughter before her older sister had wed. Jacob grudgingly agreed to be Leah's husband and to work yet another seven years in order to marry his true love, Rachel.

The ideal of marrying for love did not become generally accepted in western culture until the late Middle Ages. A form of literature became popular within the courts of Europe, consisting of tales about gallant men who served the women they loved (who, more often than not, were already married to other men). In addition, stories were created about young couples who defied the arranged marriage plans of their parents and sacrificed all in order to marry for love.

Since that time—in Western culture at least—romantic love has been regarded as the only pure and selfless basis for marriage.

In more recent times, love has come to be regarded as a basis for divorce, as well. If a couple fall in love, they get married. If they fall out of love, or if one of them falls in love with someone else, they get divorced.

In biblical days, love was something that developed for a lucky couple after they had already married each other for other reasons. Nor was it regarded as crass for a couple (and their families) to consider the question of the financial security before marriage.

Given the fact that almost 50 percent of American marriages end in dissolution, perhaps it is time to re-examine our own courtship customs in contrast to those in biblical times. For example, although modern Western society views the practice of arranged marriages with disdain, nonetheless ancient Hebrew practices may remind us how important the opinions and support of family members can be in the process of selecting a marriage partner.

The biblical examples also may challenge the popular notion that love alone is an adequate basis for marriage. Marrying for money is not respected in our culture (envied, perhaps, but not respected), yet financial stress within a marriage can do irreparable harm even to a relationship built on love. Carefully considering both persons' financial resources before seriously discussing marriage may be less crass and more healthy than many people admit.

Moreover, discovering the variety of motives in choosing marriage partners found among biblical figures is helpful in another way: it prompts us to make a personal inventory of our own oftentimes diverse motives and thereby increase our self-awareness.

Questions for Discussion

1. To what extent should parents and society have a voice in the selection of one's marriage partner?

2. What are the advantages of arranged marriages? The disadvantages?

3. If falling in love is a reason to get married, should falling out of love be a reason to get a divorce?

4. Is it realistic to appreciate sex appeal within marriage but regard it as a poor criterion in selecting a marriage partner?

5. To what extent should economic concerns and religious convictions enter into the matter of selecting a marriage partner?

6. Do parents always look after their children's best interests?

4

Multiple Marriage Models
in the Bible

Many people have the mistaken idea that the Bible presents only *one* model for marriage, a style that is amazingly similar to our own ideal. Such an assumption is soon dispelled if we set aside our own concept of matrimony and observe the practices of those fascinating people whose stories are preserved within the scriptures.

Indeed, if we ask the Bible simply to provide us with a description of marriage, we will be presented with not just one but seven different models for our consideration!

Although these seven styles are not mutually exclusive, they are distinct and different from one another. For example, a patriarchal form of marriage might also be polygamous (but not necessarily so). Even though more than one of the seven distinct styles could be found within a single marriage, nonetheless they do offer us a wondrous variety of human experiments in marital commitment and intimacy.

As we identify these styles, however, we will discover two very disturbing facts: (1) Most churches and religious writers recommend one specific style among the seven, claiming that it is the only one that is ordained by God for all couples; however, that same model is the only one of the seven that the scriptures themselves present as cursed! (2) In addition, we will also find that the specific model upon which both Jesus and Paul based their teachings regarding marriage is the one among the seven that is least understood by most Christians.

In this chapter we examine five of the seven styles. The last two—the one that is most often recommended and the one that is least understood—are discussed in the next chapter.

Polygyny

The first style is the form of marriage in which a man has two or more wives.

Polygamy can refer either to a man who has more than one wife or to a woman who has more than one husband. The only form of polygamy found in the scriptures, however, is that of polygyny (pa-LI-ja-nee), in which one man has more than one wife. No example of the opposite form, polyandry (po-lee-AN-dree), in which a woman has more than one husband, is recorded in the Bible.

There are numerous examples of polygyny in the Old Testament. Abraham had Sarah and the concubine Hagar (Genesis 16), Jacob had Leah and Rachel (Genesis 29:15–30), and Elkanah had Hannah and Peninnah (1 Samuel 1:2). Esau had at least three wives (Genesis 26:34; 36:2; 28:9), David had at least eight wives (1 Samuel 18:17–30; 25:38–43; 2 Samuel 3:2–5, 14; 11:3), Gideon had "many wives" and one concubine (Judges 8:30–31), Rehoboam had eighteen wives and sixty concubines (2 Chronicles 11:21), and Solomon had more than seven hundred wives and three hundred concubines (1 Kings 11:3)!

As startling as it may seem to us, polygyny was instituted for the benefit not of men, but of women. If a high percentage of the men in a particular society have been killed in war, or if many of the men are too poor to support wives and families, then a significant proportion of women in that society will not be able to marry and bear children—at least as long as monogamy is the only marriage option.

As the psalmist reported regarding war,

Fire devoured their young men,
    and their girls had no marriage song.

                                Psalm 78:63

Therefore, the custom developed in many cultures for wealthier men to marry more than one woman.

Polygyny, then, was a form of marriage based primarily upon economics. It was a model designed for difficult times. The practice of polygyny arose out of concern and compassion for young women who would otherwise remain dependent upon their aging parents and other relatives or else be forced to enter into prostitution or slavery. The notable exception to this usual basis for polygyny was the practice by kings (such as Solomon) of marrying foreign princesses in order to establish international trade agreements.

Two laws in the Old Testament provide some restrictions on polygyny. One makes it a capital offense for a man to marry both a woman and her mother (Leviticus 20:14). The other states that a man who marries a second wife may not "diminish the food, clothing, or marital rights of the first wife" (Exodus 21:10).

The major drawback to polygamy has always been the likelihood of jealousy arising among (in the case of polygyny) the man's wives. One memorable example of this potential problem is found in the tragic story of the two wives of Jacob, his cousins Leah and Rachel.

As we have already noted, Jacob loved Rachel but he did not have enough to pay the bride-price to her father, Laban. So Jacob provided Laban with seven years of labor for the privilege of marrying her. However, on their wedding night, after the wine had been consumed and the lights extinguished, Laban sent Rachel's older sister, Leah, into the bed chamber.

The next morning, after Jacob discovered this substitution, he was told by Uncle Laban that it was the custom for the older sister in a family to be married first. So Jacob reluctantly agreed to work another seven years as his bride-price for Rachel.

Leah, knowing that Jacob loved Rachel and did not love her, tried to win his affections by bearing children for him, expressing after each birth the longing hope, "surely now my husband will love me" (Genesis 29:32; see 29:34; 30:20).

Soon Rachel and her older sister became bitter rivals for Jacob's affections, each trying to outdo the other in bearing children. In their intense competition, each woman went so far as to enlist her female slave as a surrogate mother that in order to bear additional children by Jacob on that wife's behalf!

The potential problem of competition and jealousy among the wives of one man may have contributed to the insistence within the pastoral letters of the New Testament that a male church leader be "the husband of one wife" (1 Timothy 3:2, 12; Titus 1:6, NRSV variant).[1]

In spite of the risk of domestic rivalry and infighting, polygyny is still practiced in some cultures today. A major in the Thai army, who was married to five women at one time, informed an American acquaintance that the ideal number of wives for a man is four. "One is clearly not enough," he declared, "and two will argue and fight. A man should have his third wife picked out before marrying the second one. Four is about right. Five, on the other hand, is too many."

In most Western societies the practice of polygamy is illegal. People in those societies that do allow polygamy sometimes argue that we in the West practice polygamy without recognizing it. They point out that it is not uncommon in our culture for a person to marry, divorce, and remarry several times, for another person to live with first one sexual partner and then another, or for a married person to have an affair. All of these sexual/marital configurations, we are told, are not unlike polygamy.

"Serial marriages *is* polygamy," claimed a Lebanese I once knew, "only it is full of heartbreak and ill will. The way we do it is better and kinder. No one becomes a loser."

Concubinage

We frequently read in the Hebrew Bible, the Old Testament, of men who had one or more concubines. This marriage model too is based on economic disparity. If a woman's parents could not afford to provide a dowry, she probably would not be able to marry; however, she might become a concubine. Concubinage (kon-KYU-bin-ij) was for the daughters of the poor (including daughters of slaves).

In one sense, a concubine was a wife-for-hire. Her relationship was certainly less secure than that of a wife. Many concubines began as the servants of wives who, discovering that they themselves were barren, requested that their servants assume the role of surrogate mothers.

However, if a man fathered children by his wife as well as by a concubine, then the latter—even a firstborn son—normally would not inherit. This often led to hostility between male heirs and their halfbrothers who were born of the father's concubines. Abimelech, the son of Gideon's concubine, for example, attacked and slaughtered seventy of the sons of his father's many wives (Judges 9).

This concubinage marriage model was not restricted to Hebrew society. The Code of Hammurabi, that famous Babylonian collection of legal maxims composed some eighteen centuries before Christ, mentions the practice of concubinage in two sections. The first one concerns itself with a man whose "priestess-wife" has not borne him any children. If he wishes to take a votaress (a woman who has taken a sacred vow) as his concubine, the law states he is allowed to do so; the Code adds, however, that "this votaress shall not make herself equal with the priestess-wife" (paragraph 145). On the other hand, if he has already fathered children by a concubine who is his wife's servant, he may not then take a votaress as an additional concubine (paragraph 144).

In the second section concerning concubinage (paragraph 170), the Code of Hammurabi addresses the problem of inheritance:

> If a citizen whose wife has borne him children and [also] his bondmaid has borne his children, [and] the father during his lifetime has said to the bondmaid's children, which she has borne him, "My children"; he has added them to the children of the wife. After the father goes to his fate, the children of the wife shall divide the property of the father's house equally with the sons of the bondmaid; the son and heir, the son of the wife, shall choose a share [first] and take it.[2]

Note that although children of the man's concubine may inherit as if they were the offspring of his wife, nonetheless the principal heir, the "firstborn," is always a son of the wife, never a son of a concubine.

This matter of inheritance by the children of concubines has contributed to hostilities between Arabs and Jews, because Ishmael, Abraham's first son, is regarded as the ancestor of the Arabs. Ishmael had been born to Sarah's slave, an Egyptian woman named Hagar who had served as a surrogate mother on behalf of Sarah while she and Abraham were still childless. However, in her old age Sarah herself gave birth to a son, Isaac. The story of the ensuing rivalry is told in Genesis 21.

On the day that Isaac was weaned, Abraham ordered that a great feast be prepared. During the celebration, however, Sarah saw young Ishmael playing with her own beloved baby. "Cast out this slave woman with her son," she demanded of Abraham privately. "The son of this slave woman shall not inherit along with my son Isaac."

Abraham was very distressed over this matter, because Ishmael too was his son. However, God said to Abraham, "whatever Sarah says to you, do as she tells you." God went on to explain that Ishmael too would become the father of a nation.

So Hagar and her son were sent out into the hostile desert of Beer-sheba. When the slave woman and Ishmael finished the water they had with them, she placed the child in the shadow of a bush and walked out of sight, not wanting to witness the boy's death. There she collapsed, sobbing.

However, an angel called to the woman. "What troubles you?" the angel asked. "Do not be afraid; for God has heard the voice of the boy where he is. Come, lift up the boy and hold him fast with your hand, for I will make a great nation of him." Then God revealed to her the location of a well of water.

Hagar and Ishmael lived and eventually she got a wife for him from the land of Egypt.

As this account demonstrates, concubines were not afforded adequate social status or legal protection. This fact is even more graphically illustrated in the grisly story of a man from the tribe of Levi who, along with his concubine, became the guest of an elderly man of Gibeah (Judges 19:22–24):

> While they were enjoying themselves, the men of the city, a perverse lot, surrounded the house, and started pounding on the door. They said to the old man, the master of the house, "Bring out the man who came into your house, so that we may have intercourse with him." And the man, the master of the house, went out to them and said to them, "No, my brothers, do not act so wickedly. Since this man is my guest, do not do this vile thing. Here are my virgin daughter and his concubine; let me bring them out now. Ravish them and do whatever you want to them; but against this man do not do such a vile thing."

However, the men would not listen to him. So the Levite seized his concubine and pushed her out the door. The men gang-raped her and abused her all through the night. At dawn, the concubine fell down at the door of the old man's house.

Later, when the Levite got up and prepared to leave, he opened the door and found his concubine lying there, with her hands on the threshold.

> "Get up," he said to her, "we are going." But there was no answer. Then he put her on the donkey; and the man set out for his home. When he had entered his house, he took a knife, and grasping his concubine he cut her into twelve pieces, limb by limb, and sent her throughout all the territory of Israel. Then he commanded the men whom he sent, saying, "Thus shall you say to all the Israelites, 'Has such a thing ever happened since the day that the Israelites came up from the land of Egypt until this day? Consider it, take counsel, and speak out.'"
>
> Judges 19:28–30

Even by dismembering the corpse of his concubine and sending its various parts to other tribes of Israel, the Levite was barely able to muster an adequate number of vigilantes to inflict revenge upon the men of Gibeah and their kinsmen from the tribe of Benjamin. We must not let the gruesome details of this event obscure the more basic fact that a man's concubine was not only a wife-for-hire, but a disposable one as well. A concubine enjoyed few legal rights.

The ancient practice of concubinage has no direct modern counterpart, but certain elements of it are included within cohabitation patterns in today's society. Many couples choose to "live together" without being legally married, providing a relationship that is an alternative to legal matrimony. Often couples choose this style of relationship because they have seen their parents or other couples go through bitter and hurtful divorces, and they have become wary of the legal entanglements of marriage. Other couples choose this kind of relationship in order to avoid paying higher taxes.

However, as with the concubine of old, a couple who choose simply to "live together" may also forfeit some protection that laws provide for married people and their children.

Some people equate having a mistress as the modern counterpart of concubinage. However, concubinage was regarded as permissible in ancient societies, whereas marital infidelity, although a frequent occurrence in our own culture, is not respected.

Mutually enhancing careers

This model is based upon materialistic advantages to husband and wife. A blueprint for this model is included in the last chapter of Proverbs (31). It depicts a wife who "is far more precious than jewels." Why is she of such value to her mate? Because "the heart of her husband trusts in her, /*and he will have no lack of gain*" (verse 11, italics mine). Not only does this man's wife make clothing and buy food, she also engages in real estate transactions, a viniculture business, and a cottage industry:

> She considers a field and buys it;
>   with the fruit of her hands she plants a vineyard.
> She girds herself with strength,
>   and makes her arms strong.
> She perceives that her merchandise is profitable.
>   Her lamp does not go out at night.
> She puts her hands to the distaff,
>   and her hands hold the spindle....
> She makes linen garments and sells them;
>   she supplies the merchant with sashes....
> She looks well to the ways of her household,
>   and does not eat the bread of idleness.
>   Proverbs 31:16–19, 24, 27

Both the husband and the children of this woman praise her for her industriousness. Her earning power allows her husband to be "known in the city gates, /taking his seat among the elders of the land" (verse 23). Her productivity supports him as he exercises his respected and coveted role in the community.

In a high percentage of marriages today both the husband and the wife earn incomes. Many such couples regard this arrangement as a financial necessity. The fortunate ones also find additional enjoyment in their labors, besides that satisfaction that comes from earning money.

Some couples, however, regard marriage itself as primarily a means of furthering their own financial goals. Being married enables such a couple to advance professionally. The main goal of their marriage is economic in nature, and the success of their marriage is measured by the number and value of fine things that they can acquire, by their career satisfaction, and by their social prestige.

Law-centered marriage

In this model, the relationship of husband and wife is centered upon a legal contract, rather than being based on love, money, children, or careers. David chose to have this kind of marriage relationship with Michal, King Saul's daughter (1 Samuel 18:20–29).

Their story began when Michal fell in love with David. Her father decided to use her love as a snare to destroy David. First, Saul assured David that he would become Saul's son-in-law. The king then instructed his servants to speak privately to David, encouraging him to become Saul's son-in-law (the marriage is always referred to with that phrase, "becoming Saul's son-in-law," as if David's and Michal's relationship was only incidental). David demurred, reminding the royal servants that he was a poor man of no repute.

Saul instructed his servants to tell David that the king did not demand a monetary bride-price. Instead, all he wanted were the foreskins of one hundred of Israel's enemies, the Philistines. Saul was confident that attempting to kill and mutilate that many men would result in David's death.

David, however, was delighted with this opportunity to become the king's son-in-law. With the help of his men, David was able to slay the required number of Philistines:

> …David brought their foreskins, which were given in full number to the king, that he might become the king's son-in-law. Saul gave him his daughter Michal as a wife. But when

Saul realized that the LORD was with David, and that Saul's daughter Michal loved him, Saul was still more afraid of David. So Saul was David's enemy from that time forward.

1 Samuel 18:27b–29

When the relationship between David and Saul further eroded and David went into hiding, Saul gave Michal to another man, named Palti(el)(1 Samuel 25:44).

Later, after David had married another woman and then became king, he demanded that Michal be returned to him. After all, she was still his wife, because he had paid an agreed-upon bride-price for her. When David's officers came to take Michal away from her new husband, we read that Paltiel "went with her, weeping as he walked behind her all the way to Bahurim" (2 Samuel 3:16a).

The subsequent relationship between David and Michal is illustrated in an exchange between them on the occasion when David brought the ark of the Lord into Jerusalem. In a moment of revelry and abandon, King David danced down the streets of Jerusalem wearing little more than a beard and a grin. When he arrived at his home, Michal rebuked him with sarcasm for making such a spectacle of himself: "How the king of Israel honored himself today, uncovering himself today before the eyes of his servants' maids, as any vulgar fellow might shamelessly uncover himself!" (2 Samuel 6:20b).

David swore that he was dancing before God, who had made him king of Israel after removing her father from the throne. Then David glared angrily at Michal and declared, "I will make myself yet more contemptible than this, and I will be abased in my own eyes; but by the maids of whom you have spoken, by them I shall be held in honor" (6:22).

The storyteller summarizes the marriage relationship between David and Michal from that day on with this terse report: "And Michal the daughter of Saul had no child to the day of her death" (6:23).

Later, in the Gospels, we read of Jesus being confronted several times with questions concerning marriage, but all of these inquiries have to do with legal issues: under what circumstances is divorce permissible? What punishment shall be imposed upon this woman who committed adultery? If a woman is the widow of seven brothers, whose wife will she be after the resurrection?

Since the overarching concern of the Pharisees was obedience to *torah*, the law, it is not surprising that they—and those whom they influenced—tended to regard marriage as first and foremost a legal matter.

Many churches in our own age interpret the scriptures relating to marriage according to a legalistic question: What is or is not permissible for Christians? When ecclesiastical bodies enact rules regarding weddings and matrimony, they (like the Pharisees of old) usually do so from the perspective of the legal contract model of marriage.

Patriarchy

This model is based upon parenting, since a man cannot become a patriarch unless he fathers at least one male child.

The patriarch of the family was similar to the CEO of a modern corporation. His task was to oversee the family's labors, make major decisions, serve as the family's representative within the larger society, and defend the family's honor. His wife's role was to bear children and to be a mother.

Inherent within the patriarchal system was an unequal favoritism toward children. Abraham, for example, favored Isaac, who was regarded as his firstborn, even though he had already sired Ishmael, who was born of a concubine.

> Abraham gave all he had to Isaac. But to the sons of his concubines Abraham gave gifts, while he was still living, and he sent them away from his son Isaac, eastward to the east country.
> Genesis 25:5–6

Usually it was the eldest son whom the patriarch would eventually name as the family's new patriarch. The transfer of responsibility and power was signified by a special rite, in which the father would lay his hands upon his eldest son and bless him.

Parental favoritism often promoted jealousy and infighting among sons within a patriarchal family, as demonstrated by the rivalry of Isaac's twin sons, Esau and Jacob. The story of their conflict illustrates the nature of the patriarch's blessing and its value for the favored son. It illustrates also the manipulative and devious efforts on the part of a patriarch's wife in attempting to impose her own will upon her husband.

Isaac favored Esau, the firstborn of the two, because he was an excellent hunter and cook; he would bring down game with his bow and then prepare the meat with savory spices for his father. Rebekah, on the other hand, favored Jacob, a quiet man who stayed at home (Genesis 25:27–28).

The conflict escalated when Esau married two Hittite women (the Hittites, centered in what is now the central plateau area of Turkey, exercised considerable control over Canaan). These two wives of Esau "made life bitter for Isaac and Rebekah" (Genesis 26:35). Although the storyteller does not elaborate on her motives, we may surmise that Rebekah did not relish the idea of Esau becoming the new patriarch, not only because she favored Jacob, but also because the status of Esau's wives would thereby be elevated. So when the time came for the patriarchal blessing of the eldest son, Rebekah secretly took charge (Genesis 27).

Blind Isaac asked Esau to shoot some game and prepare it in a savory manner, then serve it to Isaac in preparation for the patriarchal blessing. Rebekah overheard these instructions. As soon as Esau had gathered up his bow and a quiver of arrows, their mother took Jacob aside. She reported the arrangements Isaac had requested.

"My son, obey my word as I command you," she ordered "Go to the flock, and get me two choice kids, so that I may prepare from them savory food for your father, such as he likes; and you shall take it to your father to eat, so that he may bless *you* before he dies."

Jacob did not hesitate to question the morality of this ruse. His only concern was its chance of success. "Look," he pointed out, "my brother Esau is a hairy man, and I am a man of smooth skin. Perhaps my father will feel me, and I shall seem to be mocking him, and bring a curse on myself and not a blessing."

His mother said to him, "Let your curse be on me, my son; only obey my word, and go, get them for me."

The deception was elaborately prepared. Rebekah dressed Jacob with some of Esau's clothing. She fastened strips of hide from a kid around his hands and his neck.

The ruse worked. Isaac, at first suspicious, finally pronounced a patriarchal blessing upon the son whom he thought was Esau. His words bequeathed two blessings: control of the household wealth and authority over other members of the family:

"May God give you of the dew of heaven,
    and of the fatness of the earth,
    and plenty of grain and wine.
Let peoples serve you,
    and nations bow down to you.
Be lord over your brothers,
    and may your mother's sons bow down to you.
Cursed be everyone who curses you,
    and blessed be everyone who blesses you!"

Genesis 27:28–29

When Esau returned and the deception was discovered, he begged Isaac to give him a blessing as well (that is, make him copatriarch with Jacob). Isaac refuses to consider such an arrangement. Instead, Isaac compromises by giving Esau permission to rebel against Jacob's rule.

Then his father Isaac answered him:
"See, away from the fatness of the earth shall your home be,
    and away from the dew of heaven on high.
By your sword you shall live,
    and you shall serve your brother;
but when you break loose,
    you shall break his yoke from your neck."

Genesis 27:39–40

The storyteller concludes this incident by emphasizing the intense feelings that the patriarchal system created among these two brothers:

Now Esau hated Jacob because of the blessing with which
his father had blessed him, and Esau said to himself, "The
days of mourning for my father are approaching; then I will
kill my brother Jacob."

Genesis 27:41

In spite of the problem of sibling jealousy and infighting,
the practice of patriarchy remained widespread and survived
for many centuries.

In medieval Europe patriarchy continued through the legal
principle of *primogeniture* (literally, "the firstborn"), in which
the eldest son inherited the family estate while the younger sons
became soldiers, sailors, merchants, craftsmen, bandits, or priests.
The Black Plague, which eliminated up to a third of the population within some countries, disrupted this practice of primogeniture. Often no heirs were left to a family, so many large
estates were eventually broken up and sold to members of the
rising middle class.

After the Industrial Revolution, more and more men found
employment at some distance from their residences, causing
them to spend full days in mines, factories, or offices—away
from family and home. With this change a new form of patriarchy was established. In it, a husband retained a kind of "absen-
tee rule" over his family, while at the same time depending on
his wife to manage their home and to care for and educate their
children. Instead of simply blessing their eldest sons, many of
these patriarchs of industry would pass on vocational skills or
businesses to their male heirs.

The patriarchal model of marriage is rarely encountered in
our contemporary society. A kind of marital relationship that is
sometimes labeled as "patriarchal" perhaps is better designated as
the traditional marriage model (described in the next chapter).

The five models listed above are presented in the scriptures
as real examples of marriage arrangements. The problems of
jealousy between wives or between sons and of the unfair treatment of concubines and their children are openly described.
None of the models described in this chapter are presented in

the Bible as God-ordained. God is described as working within these models (as in his promise to care for Hagar and his blessings upon Jacob), but not one of these five models is lifted up as the one especially favored by God.

The two remaining models of marriage, however, are not presented in a spiritually neutral manner.

Notes

[1] This phrase may mean that a church leader cannot have been divorced or widowed and then remarried. A similar phrase, "the wife of one husband" (NRSV variant), is used in 1 Timothy 5:9 regarding the requirements for a woman to be enrolled as a widow, indicating that polyandry was practiced by some members of the church or else that a woman who had been married more than once could not be enrolled as a widow. The NRSV translates both of these phrases, "married only once."

[2] Trans. by D. Winton Thomas, *Documents from Old Testament Times* (Nelson, 1958).

Questions for Discussion

1. An unhappily married man in one society secretly has a mistress. An unhappily married man in a different society brings a second wife into his home. What are the advantages and disadvantages of one situation over the other?

2. In the story of the Levite's concubine, her death is avenged by other Israelites. However, the man's own action of pushing her out into a mob in order to protect himself receives no censure. To what extent can laws protect unmarried sexual partners from failing to protect each other? To what extent can laws protect married couples from failing to protect each other?

3. Is the mutually enhancing careers model of marriage likely to provide maximum satisfaction to husband and wife? Why or why not?

4. What difference would it make if the preacher or the counselor regarded marriage as primarily a legal contract (as opposed to a relational view of marriage)?

5. Which class or group within our own society would benefit most from a revival of the patriarchal form of marriage and family life?

5

Two Other Models—
One Blessed, the Other Cursed

Of the seven biblical models of marriage, the two remaining ones are found in the book of Genesis. They differ from the other five in that they are reported as having been instituted by God: one as a curse, the other as a blessing.

The traditional marriage model

The first of these may best be called the traditional marriage model. It is described in Genesis 3:8–19, in the words of God to Adam and Eve after they had eaten the forbidden fruit:

> They heard the sound of the LORD God walking in the garden at the time of the evening breeze, and the man and his wife hid

65

themselves from the presence of the LORD God among the trees of the garden. But the LORD God called to the man, and said to him, "Where are you?" He said, "I heard the sound of you in the garden, and I was afraid, because I was naked; and I hid myself." He said, "Who told you that you were naked? Have you eaten from the tree of which I commanded you not to eat?" The man said, "The woman whom you gave to be with me, she gave me fruit from the tree, and I ate." Then the LORD God said to the woman, "What is this that you have done?" The woman said, "The serpent tricked me, and I ate." The LORD God said to the serpent,

> "Because you have done this,
>> cursed are you among all animals
>> and among all wild creatures;
> upon your belly you shall go,
>> and dust you shall eat
>> all the days of your life.
> I will put enmity between you and the woman,
>> and between your offspring and hers;
> he will strike your head,
>> and you will strike his heel."

To the woman he said,

> "I will greatly increase your pangs in childbearing;
>> in pain you shall bring forth children,
> yet your desire shall be for your husband,
>> and he shall rule over you."

And to the man he said,

> "Because you have listened to the voice of your wife,
>> and have eaten of the tree
> about which I commanded you,
>> 'You shall not eat of it,'
> cursed is the ground because of you;
>> in toil you shall eat of it all the days of your life;
> thorns and thistles it shall bring forth for you;
>> and you shall eat the plants of the field.
> By the sweat of your face
>> you shall eat bread
> until you return to the ground,
>> for out of it you were taken;

you are dust,
and to dust you shall return."

This traditional model of marriage is based upon sin. It is the result of God's punishment of Adam and Eve for their disobedience in eating the forbidden fruit. In spite of the fact that it is grounded in guilt, this model is the one most often prescribed by churches and religious writers. They often present it as the one that God has ordained for humanity, promising that couples who pattern their marriages upon this model will be rewarded with marital happiness.

On the other hand, this same traditional model is what St. Augustine had in mind when he defined marriage as "a covenant with death."

Three characteristics of the traditional model, as defined in Genesis, seriously challenge the idea that patterning one's own marriage upon this model will insure happiness:

First, this model is centered upon pain and toil. We read that God said to Eve, "I will greatly increase your pangs in childbearing" (verse 16), and that God said to Adam, "cursed is the ground because of you; /in toil you shall eat of it all the days of your life" (verse 17). The word that is translated "pangs" and "toil" in these two verses is the same word, *'eseb*. It means both "pain" and "labor." It describes Eve's anguish when bearing children and it describes Adam's exhaustion when tilling the ground.

The traditional model of marriage, therefore, is centered on painful labor—labor in birthing that is cursed with additional agony, and labor in tilling soil that is cursed with many thorns and thistles.

Second, in this traditional model the husband and wife want to control each other. Eve was told, "your desire shall be for your husband, and he shall rule over you" (verse 16). In the English translation, it sounds as if her only desire would be to please her husband. However, the word in Hebrew that is translated "desire," *teshuqah*, is neither a pleasant nor a romantic word. The meaning of *teshuqah* is demonstrated in the following chapter in Genesis, when God speaks to Cain (4:6–7):

> The LORD said to Cain, "Why are you angry, and why has your countenance fallen? If you do well, will you not be accepted? And if you do not do well, sin is lurking at the door; its *desire* is for you, but you must master it." [Italics mine.]

Teshuqah, then, is an insatiable desire to control a person. Eve was told that Adam would rule over her and that she would "desire" him—meaning that she would want to control him. He would be domineering, yes, but she would be manipulative and cunning and charming. Each of them would try to control the other.

This desire to control one's marriage partner is further emphasized by a pun in the Hebrew text. In verse 10 the author states that Adam and Eve, having eaten the forbidden fruit, realize that they are naked. The word for naked in this verse is *'erom*. It is a pun on another word, *'arum*, used in verse 1 to describe the serpent who tempted them. *'Arum* means "crafty" or "sly" or "cunning." By using these sound-alike words, the writer implies that Adam and Eve have now become like the serpent, the tempter, trying to entice and control each other.

Moreover, notice that even the use of pronouns changes from *we* in verse 2 to *I* in verse 10.

> Now the serpent was more crafty than any other wild animal that the LORD God had made. He said to the woman, "Did God say, 'You shall not eat from any tree in the garden'?" The woman said to the serpent, "We may eat of the fruit of the trees in the garden...."
>
> Genesis 3:1–2

> But the LORD God called to the man, and said to him, "Where are you?" He said, "I heard the sound of you in the garden, and I was afraid, because I was naked; and I hid myself."
>
> Genesis 3:9–10

Although the commandment not to eat of the fruit had been given only to Adam, before Eve's creation, she nonetheless referred to the two of them as a unity, as "we." After the fall, however, Adam spoke only of himself. Although both the man and the woman hide from God, nonetheless their sense of unity is lost. Adam's answer referred only to himself: "I heard…I was afraid…I was naked…I hid myself." He then went on to blame Eve for his miserable self-loathing.

This leads to the third characteristic of the traditional model of marriage, "blame-dropping." When Adam and Eve experienced a sense of guilt and fear, their first response is to blame someone else. God confronted Adam, asking if he had eaten of the forbidden fruit, and Adam answered: "The *woman* whom *you* gave to be with me, *she* gave me fruit from the tree…." (verse 12, emphasis mine). It was all Eve's fault, according to Adam. Ultimately, however, it was all God's fault, Adam insisted, because it was God who gave him the *woman*.

About a hundred years ago, many fundamentalist Christians began to preach that the traditional model of marriage, based on God's words to Adam and Eve after the fall, is binding upon all Christians. The husband, they taught, is supposed to rule over his wife. The wife, they insisted, is supposed to love and obey her husband and to bear many children. Some individuals even objected to the use of painkillers during childbirth, claiming that it violated God's intention that a woman bear children "in pain." (None of them objected to the use of weed-killers, however, even though the same scripture declares that a man will encounter thorns and thistles.)

So these church leaders preached that Christians are to accept a kind of marriage that is based on punishment, arising from a curse by God, in which the husband is a tired boss at home and his wife is his obedient baby-machine.

This model was well illustrated by the fictional television character, Archie Bunker, who once told his daughter, Gloria, "Me and your mother think the same. And I know, 'cause I do her thinking for her."

The companionship model

A quite different model of marriage is based on Adam and Eve before the fall. It is described in Genesis 2:18–25 as the model that God planned for humanity before Adam and Eve messed everything up.

> Then the LORD God said, "It is not good that the man should be alone; I will make him a helper as his partner." So out of the ground the LORD God formed every animal of the field and every bird of the air, and brought them to the man to see what he would call them; and whatever the man called every living creature, that was its name. The man gave names to all cattle, and to the birds of the air, and to every animal of the field; but for the man there was not found a helper as his partner. So the LORD God caused a deep sleep to fall upon the man, and he slept; then he took one of his ribs and closed up its place with flesh. And the rib that the LORD God had taken from the man he made into a woman and brought her to the man. Then the man said,
> "This at last is bone of my bones
> and flesh of my flesh;
> this one shall be called Woman,
> for out of Man this one was taken."
> Therefore a man leaves his father and his mother and clings to his wife, and they become one flesh. And the man and his wife were both naked, and were not ashamed.

God was motivated to create the woman because he observed that "it is not good that the man should be alone" (verse 18). This model, therefore, is based upon the human need for companionship.

Centuries later the apostle Paul emphasized this need on the part of Adam in discussing the relationship of men and women in the church. He reminded the Christians in Corinth of this original model for marriage, saying that man was not "created for the sake of woman, but woman for the sake of man" (1 Corinthians 11:9). However, to correct any seeming dissimilarity between the needs of men and women, he quickly added, "Nevertheless, in the Lord woman is not independent of man or man independent of woman" (1 Corinthians 11:11).

One might suppose that Adam's need for companionship could have been satisfied by giving him a pet—perhaps a nice dog or a cat or maybe even an ape. Therefore, according to the story God brought all sorts of animals to Adam for him to name (just as people do with pets), but none of the animals satisfied Adam's deep longing for companionship.

So God created a woman. Adam studied God's handiwork. "This, at last," Adam exclaimed, admiring the woman, "is bone of my bones / and flesh of my flesh" (Genesis 2:23). Adam liked what he saw. (Apparently Eve was not too disappointed, either.)

This model of marriage, according to the author of Genesis, was God's original plan for marriage. It was what God intended for humanity. It is for this kind of relationship that a man will leave his mother and father. As with the traditional model, this one too is God-ordained. This model, however, is not imposed as a punishment; rather, it is provided as a source of companionship.

In verse 24 we read that a man "leaves" his father and mother and "clings" to his wife. Both of those words are associated with the concept of covenant. The word translated "leaves" is used elsewhere to describe the action of a person giving up worshiping idols in order to worship the living God. The word translated "clings" is used elsewhere to describe a person's willingness to remain faithful to God. The choice of these terms implies that marriage is meant to be a covenant, a deep and lasting agreement that involves the totality of two persons.

The account goes on to say that Adam and Eve were naked "and were not ashamed" (verse 25). The Hebrew word translated "naked" in this verse (*'arom*) is slightly different than the word used to describe the couple after they had sinned. Moreover, the statement that they were not ashamed implies that Adam and Eve were open to each other, innocent and trusting. They were exposed to each other, without fear of criticism or rejection.

Unlike after the fall, Adam and Eve began their relationship as equals. Their equality is indicated in the two terms God used to describe Eve. God said that the woman would be for Adam "a helper as his partner" (verse 18). Older translations render the Hebrew as "a help meet for him" (KJV), "a helper suitable for him" (NASB; NIV), or, "a helper fit for him" (RSV).

English-speaking readers might think that describing Eve as Adam's "helper" implies that she was inferior to him, that she was his servant or aide. The Hebrew, however, does not carry this sense of subordination or subservience. The word that is translated "helper" is *ezer,* and *ezer* does not denote a person of lower status. That fact is dramatically demonstrated by the way *ezer* is used in the rest of the Old Testament. Four times *ezer* describes military leaders and allies; the thirteen other times it is used in the Hebrew Bible it describes God himself!

The second word, translated as "meet," "suitable," or "fit," is *knegdwo.* It is based on the term *neged,* which refers to what is "in front of" or "corresponding to." This word also does not imply inferiority or inequality. Quite the opposite! A related word, *nagid,* refers to a leader, a ruler, a prince, a king, or an overseer. It was used to describe Saul, David, and Solomon as monarchs (1 Samuel 9:16; 13:14; 1 Kings 1:35).

In describing Eve, both a prefix and a suffix are attached to *neged.* The prefix, *k,* indicates a comparison or similarity. Hence, the first two parts of the word, *knegd-,* means "corresponding to." The suffix, *wo,* says that the word it is attached to refers to "him."

Therefore, describing Eve as *knegdwo* means that Eve was similar to Adam. She was "equal and adequate to himself."[1] One of the early church fathers, Irenaeus, in referring to the meaning of *knegdwo,* said that God made "a helper equal and the peer and like of Adam."

By choosing his words carefully, the author of Genesis has clearly indicated that Adam was not the boss. Neither was Eve. They were marriage "partners"—before the fall, at least.

Summary and analysis

Two different models for marriage are exemplified in the second and third chapters of Genesis. The traditional model, prescribed by fundamentalist Christians, is based on punishment and pain. It is characterized by a desire to control one's marriage partner, to lay blame on someone else when troubles occur, and to assign distinct roles: husbands are to toil outside the home and wives are to bear children in pain.

Those who advocate this model today often point out that it came directly from God. They fail to mention that it was given as a curse, the result of human sin! By their insistence that this model is for all Christians, they imply that Christ's coming did nothing to remove the curse. Although our souls may be redeemed, their interpretation suggests that our marriages may not.

If one argues that the traditional model came directly from God, the same may be said for the companionship model, the original one. This model does not demand that a couple have children, or that husband and wife perform distinct roles, or that one rules over the other. Instead, the wording implies that Adam and Eve were engaged in the same activities together as partners.

Moreover, this original model does not arise from human sin, but from human innocence.

Therefore, if Christ has secured for us grace and mercy, if we have been forgiven and saved, if the curse is lifted on our behalf, then surely this first model of marriage is now open to us.

Jesus implied that this was indeed so. Whenever he spoke of marriage, Jesus said that the goal of a married couple is to become "one flesh," language taken directly from this portion of scripture, from this original model for marriage (verse 24).

In the same way, the apostle Paul too spoke of marriage in terms of "one flesh," implying that this original model of marriage is now open for all Christians.

However, the phrase "one flesh," used so intentionally by Jesus and by Paul as the basis for marriage, is seldom spoken from pulpits today nor is it familiar to many Christians.

Note

[1]Brown, Driver and Briggs, *A Hebrew and English Lexicon of the Old Testament* (Oxford, 1966 ed.), p. 617.

Questions for Discussion

1. Why do you think that the traditional model has been presented by so many churches and individuals as the will of God for marriages?

2. In this chapter, three characteristics of Adam and Eve's relationship after the fall are listed: their roles involve much pain and toil, they desire to control each other, and they blame others for their own sins. To what extent are these characteristics found in marriages today?

3. Could the idea that the purpose of marriage is companionship become normative in our society? Why or why not?

4. If marriage is a covenant, to what degree can the relationship be maintained by one partner without the other's active cooperation?

5. The statement is made that those who advocate the traditional model for marriages imply that Christ's coming has not effected any changes in the marriage relationship. In what ways, if any, could the gospel alter the three characteristics of the traditional model?

6

Sex and Marriage
in the Gospels

My wife and I were relaxing in the mezzanine of a hotel in Cairo, Egypt, when we heard loud, rhythmic music from the lobby. Looking down the staircase, we viewed a bride and groom (in expensive Western-style dress), with attendants and guests, being filmed with TV cameras as they slowly processed toward the stairs.

The bridal couple were preceded by six young men in traditional Egyptian garb, playing tambourines and singing what apparently were slightly ribald verses to a song. Ahead of them processed six young women, all dressed alike and carrying huge candles, symbolically lighting the way for the wedding party. I watched, fascinated at the longevity of wedding customs—for surely here, embodied in the persons of these young women, were the modern counterparts of the young women in Christ's parable about the wise and foolish maidens!

However, although nuptial practices may endure throughout the centuries, the essential meaning and purpose of marriage has not remained constant within either the church or Western civilization.

An ideal view of marriage

The Gospels and the writings of Paul (including those attributed to Paul but about which there is some doubt concerning authorship) present a single and unified understanding of the nature and purpose of marriage. This understanding, however, is rather alien to modern society. In order to understand what Jesus and Paul both claim is God's will for marriages, we must look closely at an unfamiliar phrase, "become one flesh" (Genesis 2:24), used to describe the goal of the companionship model of marriage.

Before we do, however, it is important to recognize that we are focusing our attention upon an ideal concept marriage—not a description of how marriages are, but a vision of how marriages would be at their very best.

There are many churches that regard marriage from a legalistic perspective. They make rules and pronounce judgments. They fill the air with "ought" and "should" and "must," making the teachings of Jesus into a new law, much harsher than the law of Moses.

Our Savior never flinched from teaching about the ideal way of life. He constantly lifted up the way that things were meant to be. For example, he said:

> Do not think that I have come to abolish the law or the prophets; I have come not to abolish but to fulfill. For truly I tell you, until heaven and earth pass away, not one letter, not one stroke of a letter, will pass from the law until all is accomplished.
>
> Matthew 5:17–18

Jesus wanted to preserve the ideal. He went on to warn his followers:

> Therefore, whoever annuls one of the least of these commandments, and teaches others to do the same, will be called least in the kingdom of heaven; but whoever does them and teaches them will be called great in the kingdom of heaven.
>
> Matthew 5:19

Nonetheless, Jesus regarded the law—the ideal—as subservient to human need. He healed on the sabbath, for example, which was a violation of the law. When he and his disciples were hungry, they harvested grain to eat, doing so on the sabbath and thereby violating the law. "The sabbath was made for humankind," Jesus said, "and not humankind for the sabbath" (Mark 2:27). The ideal must always be subject to human need.

Moreover, Jesus placed grace over law. One time some Pharisees brought before Jesus a woman who was guilty of adultery. According to the law, she was to be put to death for her offense:

> If a man commits adultery with the wife of his neighbor, both the adulterer and the adulteress shall be put to death.
>
> Leviticus 20:10

They asked Jesus for his opinion. He instructed them, "Let anyone among you who is without sin be the first to throw a stone at her" (John 8:7). After all of the good law-and-order Pharisees had slunk away, Jesus turned to the woman and asked if anyone condemned her. "No one, sir," she answered. Then Jesus said, "Neither do I condemn you. Go your way, and from now on do not sin again" (John 8:11).

Jesus refused to abandon the ideal. He could still speak of the woman as one who had sinned. Yet he also refused to condemn her, even though she had failed to live up to the ideal. Jesus placed grace over law. The ideal gives us direction and goal in life, but it is grace that enables us to pick ourselves up and keep on trying.

Perhaps Jesus knew that emphasizing the ideal at the expense of grace often backfires. We find this is true, even today.

For example, our Latter Day Saints friends have traditionally insisted on complete abstinence from alcoholic beverages. In Jewish culture, on the other hand, drinking in moderation is regarded as normal and acceptable. A careful study of the incidents of alcoholism among Mormons, among Jews, and among Americans as a whole revealed that, of the three groups, the highest proportion of alcoholism was found among Mormons, and the lowest percentage was found among Jews.[1]

Similarly, a study by the University of Wisconsin on religious affiliation and family beliefs concluded that "Jews are very tolerant of separation or divorce but have low rates themselves. In contrast," it added, "Baptists have high rates of marital dissolution despite very conservative beliefs on this subject."[2]

Jesus in the Gospels is portrayed as refusing to abandon the ideal or to condemn those who fail to reach it. Paul underscored that tension, stating that while "the law is holy, and the commandment is holy and just and good" (Romans 7:12), nonetheless "all have sinned and fall short of the glory of God" (Romans 3:23). We all fall short of the ideal, so we are saved not by scolding but by grace. Let us remember this as we explore the ideal model of marriage found in the teachings of Jesus.

Five female ancestors

Jesus' attitude about sexual and marital irregularities may be reflected in his genealogy as reported in the Gospel of Matthew. This list is remarkable because it includes references to several female ancestors, something not done in Jewish genealogies at that time. Not only are five women mentioned, but all of these women are associated with some form of less-than-ideal sexual behavior.[3]

The first woman mentioned is Tamar, the daughter-in-law of Judah, the childless widow who was given in levirate marriage to a brother-in-law named Onan. As we noted, Onan did not want to bear offspring for his dead brother, and so he practiced premature withdrawal during intercourse.[4] When Onan died, Judah put off Tamar's marriage to his third son (fearing that he too might die).

Tired of waiting, Tamar disguised herself as a prostitute in order to became pregnant by Judah himself. When the ruse was revealed, Judah admitted concerning Tamar, "she is more in the right than I" (Genesis 38:26).

The second woman mentioned in the genealogy is Rahab, a prostitute in Jericho. This Canaanite woman was remembered for hiding the spies sent by Joshua and allowing them to use her window as a means of escape (Joshua 2).

The third woman mentioned is Ruth, a widow from Moab. As a Moabite, according to the law, she was cursed: "No Ammonite or Moabite shall be admitted to the assembly of the LORD" (Deuteronomy 23:3).

Nonetheless Ruth is identified as the great-grandmother of King David and one of the ancestors of Jesus of Nazareth. Although she was a penniless widow and an immigrant, Ruth attracted the eye of Boaz, an older, wealthy Israelite relative of her late husband. Following the suggestion of her mother-in-law, she crept onto the threshing floor where Boaz was sleeping one night and lay down beside him, uncovering his legs (an intimate act). When he grew cold and awoke, he was surprised to find a woman next to him (Ruth 3:8). She identified herself and invited him to spread his cloak over her (an idiomatic phrase that denoted sexual intercourse/marriage). Boaz was delighted that she would approach him, an older man, with such an offer. Swearing that he would negotiate with her dead husband's kinsman for her, he urged her to stay with him for the night and to depart before dawn, lest she be seen.

The fourth woman mentioned is Bathsheba, who attracted the lustful eye of King David as he stood on the roof of his palace and watched her bathe. In this genealogy she is identified only as "the wife of Uriah," recalling to the reader's mind how David committed adultery with her and then had her husband, Uriah, killed in battle in order to cover up David and Bathsheba's sexual crime (2 Samuel 11).

The fifth woman mentioned is Mary, Jesus' mother, who became pregnant while betrothed to Joseph (Matthew 1:18–19). During the year of betrothal a couple were legally married but did not live together or engage in sexual intercourse. Theoretically, this custom was designed to insure a groom that any child born to them was his own and (if a son) had the right to inherit.

However, Mary became pregnant during this period. According to the law, she deserved the death penalty:

> If there is a young woman, a virgin already engaged to be married, and a man meets her in the town and lies with her, you shall bring both of them to the gate of that town and stone them to death, the young woman because she did not cry for help in the town and the man because he violated his neighbor's wife. So you shall purge the evil from your midst.
>
> Deuteronomy 22:23–24

Joseph chose instead to divorce her quietly (until he was told by an angel that she had conceived by the Holy Spirit).

Perhaps the inclusion of these five women in Matthew's version of Jesus' family tree was meant to prepare the reader for Jesus' radical opposition to the notion of women as sexual property.

Opposition to the idea of sexual property

Time and again Jesus demonstrated his respect for women as persons, not just possessions.

In the Judean society of Jesus' day a man was not to speak with a woman in public (even if she were his own wife or daughter), and never to converse with a Gentile woman. Certainly a man was not to teach a woman. Nor was a man to touch any woman other than his wife or daughter—however innocent the purpose, and especially if she were in her menstrual period.

Nonetheless, Jesus defied every one of these rules. He commended the gutsiness of a Canaanite woman's answer to his tentative refusal to provide help for her daughter (Matthew

15:21–28). He told a parable about a widow who refused to take "no" from an unjust judge (Luke 18:1–8). He gladly taught Mary and told her sister that Mary had chosen "the better part" instead of tending to "women's work" (Luke 10:38–41). He turned to a woman who had touched him (a woman suffering from continual menstrual hemorrhaging for twelve years), addressed her in public, and praised her faith (Matthew 9:20–22 and parallels).

It is interesting to note that some churches have denied women the right to come near their altar because an Old Testament law states that a menstruating woman is unclean (Leviticus 15:19–30); yet, in contrast, Jesus praised this menstruating woman who actually touched him!

Jesus objected to any attitude that regarded women as mere sex objects, condemning not only the act of adultery but even the harboring of lustful fantasies about adultery (Matthew 5:27–28).

This particular teaching against "anyone who looks at a woman with lust" needs clarification, in that it seems to be condemning normal, natural sexual urges, part of the "good" creation of God. This misunderstanding is reinforced by the use of the word "heart" in the phrase "has already committed adultery with her in his heart." We think of the "heart" as the center of human emotions. In biblical times, however, "heart" denoted that which we call the "mind." The heart was believed to be the center of one's will and intentions.

This teaching of Jesus concerning adultery contains other important nuances that are not reflected in the English translation. The wording in Greek reads, literally, "everyone seeing a woman with a view to desire her has already committed adultery with her in the heart [mind]." The phrase "with a view" is an attempt to translate the Greek word *pros*. It means "for the purpose of," "with the intention of," "toward the goal of."

Because of language differences, we who read this passage in English wonder at the impossibility of Jesus' words. In the Greek, however, Jesus' thought is clearer. He was saying, in effect, that a man who watches a woman for the intentional purpose of desiring her is already committing adultery with her in his mind. Jesus was not condemning natural sexual urges. He was condemning the attitude that regards a woman as a sexual object to be coveted and owned and used.

Nowhere is Jesus' opposition to the principle of sexual property more clearly demonstrated than in his response to a woman of ill repute who came to him during a party and washed his feet with her tears, dried them with her hair, kissed them, and anointed them with expensive perfume (Luke 7:36–50). The host, on the other hand, who was a Pharisee, saw this woman only in terms of her sexual history. In his mind she was not a person so much as "a sinner." According to the social and religious mores of his time, Jesus should have avoided looking at her, much less conversing with her; instead, he should have rebuked her severely by speaking critically about her to the other males in the room.

Instead, Jesus reacted in a shocking manner. He began by contrasting this woman's loving actions with those of his host! Not only that, but Jesus looked at the woman and spoke directly to her about her sins and her faith. Moreover, he forgave her and blessed her.

As was mentioned above, Jesus disregarded the Mosaic law even regarding a woman who was found guilty of adultery (John 8:2–11). Instead of arguing against the law, he forced each person present to acknowledge its double standard ("Let anyone among you who is without sin be the first to throw a stone at her"). Women are not more sinful than men, Jesus' words and actions imply, nor are women mere sexual possessions.

The concept of "one flesh"

One time Jesus was confronted by some Pharisees who were debating the legal question of when divorce is permissible:

> Some Pharisees came to him, and to test him they asked, "Is it lawful for a man to divorce his wife for any cause?" He

answered, "Have you not read that the one who made them
at the beginning 'made them male and female,' and said,
'For this reason a man shall leave his father and mother and
be joined to his wife, and the two shall become one flesh'? So
they are no longer two, but one flesh. Therefore what God
has joined together, let no one separate."

Matthew 19:3–6

These Pharisees were looking at marriage from the viewpoint of a legal contract. Jesus viewed marriage differently. He
regarded marriage as a relationship. His expressed concern was
not about when a marriage can end, but how a marriage can
develop. In doing so, Jesus referred these Pharisees to the language of the original marriage model, the one describing Adam
and Eve before they sinned, before their marriage changed into
what we now call the traditional model.

Jesus quoted Genesis 2:24:

Therefore a man leaves his father and his mother and clings
to his wife, and they become one flesh.

These words are at the heart of God's intention when he
made us male and female. It is our Creator's will, they tell us,
that a married couple become "one flesh." These words encap-
sulate the goal of marriage. But what do these two words mean?
How do a husband and wife become "one flesh"? By eating the
same food?

"one":

The word *one* in the New Testament is usually a numerical
term—"one person," "one hour," "one shekel." But in saying
that a married couple is to become "one flesh," Jesus did not
mean that they are to become Siamese twins! He was not using
the word *one* to indicate a number. Jesus used it to mean something quite different.

According to the Gospel of John, Christ spoke of himself
and the Father as "one" (10:30) and echoed this thought in
Gethsemane while praying for his disciples. Asking God to pro-

tect them, he added the important request that his followers "be one, as we are one" (17:11).

When Jesus utilized the word *one* in these two passages he was not praying that the number of his followers dwindle down to one single individual! He was using *one* to mean something quite different. Later in that same prayer, Jesus asked this for all of his followers,

> ...that they may all be one. As you, Father, are in me and I am in you, may they also be in us, so that the world may believe that you have sent me. The glory that you have given me I have given them, so that they may be one, as we are one, I in them and you in me, that they may become completely one, so that the world may know that you have sent me and have loved them even as you have loved me.
>
> John 17:21–23

Jesus wanted us to become "one," "completely one"—not one in number, but one through having a sense of unity, connectedness, and caring.

In Acts we read how the believers were of "one heart" (Acts 4:32), and Paul reminded his readers that they were "one body in Christ" (Romans 12:5) and that all of them—Jews and Gentiles, males and females, slaves and free people—were "one in Christ" (Galatians 3:28).

Whenever the word *one* in the New Testament is not used to denote a number, it denotes harmony, unity, and equality. That is the meaning of *one* in the phrase "one flesh."

"flesh":

The word *flesh* in English refers to a physical body. The word for body in the New Testament is *soma* (SO-ma). However, it is not *soma*, but a different word in the New Testament, *sarx* (SARKS), that is translated "flesh."

Sarx, "flesh," has several meanings, all of them shared with its Hebrew counterpart, *basar*. In the Old Testament, "flesh" often referred to the meaty portions of a physical body:

So the LORD God caused a deep sleep to fall upon the man, and he slept; then he took one of his ribs and closed up its place with flesh.

> Genesis 2:21

When referring to animals, *flesh* simply meant "meat" that may or may not be eaten. Human bodies, according to ancient Hebrew thought, are composed of flesh and three other materials:

You clothed me with skin and flesh,
  and knit me together with bones and sinews.

> Job 10:11

I looked, and there were sinews on them [bones], and flesh had come upon them, and skin had covered them; but there was no breath in them.

> Ezekiel 37:8

However, sometimes "flesh" referred to skin:

You shall not make any gashes in your flesh for the dead or tattoo any marks upon you: I am the LORD.

> Leviticus 19:28

You shall circumcise the flesh of your foreskins, and it shall be a sign of the covenant between me and you.

> Genesis 17:11

You shall make for them linen undergarments to cover their naked flesh; they shall reach from the hips to the thighs....

> Exodus 28:42

Often the word served as a general term designating all living things or human beings in particular:

And God saw that the earth was corrupt; for all flesh had corrupted its ways upon the earth. And God said to Noah, "I have determined to make an end of all flesh, for the earth is filled with violence because of them; now I am going to destroy them along with the earth.

> Genesis 6:12–13

> In God, whose word I praise,
>> in God I trust; I am not afraid;
>> what can flesh do to me?
>
> Psalm 56:4

Many times one's "flesh" meant one's biological relatives:

> ...and Laban said to him [his nephew, Jacob], "Surely you are my bone and my flesh!"
>
> Genesis 29:14a

> "Come, let us sell him to the Ishmaelites, and not lay our hands on him, for he is our brother, our own flesh." And his brothers agreed.
>
> Genesis 37:27

> ...the gospel concerning his Son, who was descended from David according to the flesh....
>
> Romans 1:3

"Flesh" also served as a symbol of a person's earthly life:

> In the days of his flesh, Jesus offered up prayers and supplications....
>
> Hebrews 5:7a

Nowhere in the Old Testament does "flesh" carry a sexual connotation, with perhaps one exception:

> I also gathered for myself silver and gold and the treasure of kings and of the provinces; I got singers, both men and women, and delights of the flesh, and many concubines.
>
> Ecclesiastes 2:8

In this passage, "delights of the flesh" may refer to sexual pleasures, since the phrase is followed by "and many concubines," but it is equally possible that it could refer to the enjoyment of music ("singers, both men and women") or serve as a collective expression for the many pleasures that life has to offer.

Therefore, *flesh* in the Old Testament is a morally neutral term. It is not a negative word. It carries no more stigma than such synonyms as *muscle tissue, relatives, lifespan, human being,* or *enjoyment.*

In the Gospels *flesh* (*sarx*) retains its character as a neutral term. *Sarx* sometimes refers to a physical body (as in 1 John 4:2), but it usually means something much broader than that. As in the Old Testament, so also in the Gospels *flesh* is not a sexual term. Instead, *sarx* denotes a person's physical and emotional being, lived out in the course of this earthly existence.

"one flesh":

Although Jesus never defined the phrase "one flesh," we can make seven important observations about that wording.

First, becoming "one flesh" is not the same as becoming "one spirit." This latter phrase would imply that two individual personalities are meant to merge into one. Some Gnostic thinkers argued that the original human, Adam, was androgynous, both male and female. Then God split Adam into two half-persons, one male and the other female. Adam recognized this when he described Eve as "bone of my bones /and flesh of my flesh" (Genesis 2:23a). Since then, according to this fanciful idea, every marriage is a reuniting, through which a man and a woman become a whole person.

The idea that an unmarried person is not a complete and whole being is foreign to the New Testament. As far as the Gospels indicate, Jesus himself was unmarried and he included a number of single persons among his followers. Paul referred to himself as single (1 Corinthians 7:7–8; 9:5) and recommended that unmarried persons remain so, given the stressful times and the fact that a married person is divided between pleasing his or her marriage partner and serving the Lord (1 Corinthians 7).

Moreover, the phrase "one in spirit" implies that two persons would remain married even after death, something that Jesus declared was impossible (Mark 12:25).

Second, saying that two people become "one flesh" does not mean that they must always agree on things. There would be other, more explicit means of saying that in the Greek of the New Testament. A couple may hold different, even conflicting opinions, not unlike the fact that an individual may have ambivalent thoughts on a subject. Differences can become an extension rather than a division, if a couple become "one flesh."

Third, saying that two persons become "one flesh" implies that they will be bonded as "one" in terms of their hopes, drives, and ambitions (*sarx*). Their lives are headed in the same direction, together.

Fourth, in becoming "one flesh," the feelings of one's marriage partner become inseparably part of one's own feelings. A stubbed toe can make one's whole body feel pain, even though one's toe is a long ways from one's brain. Our bodies are single unities. A person's brain is "one flesh" with his or her toe.

In the same way, a husband and wife are meant to reach a point where communication is so good that one feels the other's pain and joy as quickly as one's own. A husband and wife are to be connected in their hearts and minds, just as members of one's body are interconnected.

If a couple become "one flesh," then a husband would be as hesitant to hurt his wife as he would be to hurt himself, and a wife would be as hesitant to hurt her husband as she would be to hurt herself.

Fifth, the concept of two persons becoming "one" rules out any idea that a marriage is composed of a superior over an inferior, or that the needs and choices and ambitions of one are more important than the needs and choices and ambitions of the other. "The two shall become one" does not require the question, "which one?" They do not become one person or one spirit; they only become "one flesh."

Jesus treated both singles and married people as individuals in their own right. Similarly, when Paul suggested that a believing person may become the source of salvation for his or her unbelieving partner, he thereby acknowledged both the individuality of marriage partners and the effect one may have upon the other (1 Corinthians 7:14).

Sixth, becoming "one flesh" is a process. The construction of the phrase "the two shall become one" implies that doing so requires time and experience. The same troubles may drive some couples apart and other couples closer together. Perhaps allowing difficulties to bring a married couple closer together is part of becoming "one flesh."

Seventh, becoming "one flesh" has a spiritual dimension. Jesus said, "What God has joined together, let no one separate" (Mark 10:9). In objecting to the divorce laws in his own society, Jesus did not appeal to the extreme unfairness to women but to the way that popular attitudes about marriage thwarted God's role in strengthening the marriage bond. (See Chapter 8.)

Notes

[1] One explanation for this disproportion may be the "forbidden fruit" appeal. A more practical explanation was given by a student at Brigham Young University: "When you have to drive forty miles for a drink, you don't stop with just one."

[2] Quoted in Martin E. Marty's *Context* in the publication *Salt* (date unknown).

[3] For a fuller discussion of possible reasons for the inclusion of these women in Matthew's genealogy of Jesus, see Raymond Brown, "Why the Women?" *The Birth of the Messiah* (NY: Doubleday, 1977, 1993), pp. 71–74.

[4] The subsequent use of the story of Onan by church leaders to establish the "wrongness" of masturbation is unfounded, since his sin was not in "spilling his seed" *per se*, but in failing to impregnate Tamar.

Questions for Discussion

1. Is it practical—or even possible—to relate to others with a sense of grace and still maintain one's ideals?

2. In the story of the woman accused of adultery, why was only she and not also her sexual partner brought out to be stoned to death? Has the "sexual revolution" in our society eliminated a double standard for sexual misconduct?

3. Why is it often difficult to relate to a particularly immoral individual as a person rather than as a "sinner" or "criminal"?

4. The word translated "flesh" means not only one's body, but also one's feelings, ambitions, personality, and life experiences. In which of these is it easy for a couple to become "one flesh"? In which is it especially difficult?

5. In this chapter it was suggested that difficult times can drive a couple apart or bring them closer together. If this is true, what qualities will make the difference?

7

Sex and Marriage in the Early Church

Was Jesus' ideal description of marriage, "one flesh," retained and made normative within the early church? Yes, by Paul at least—but with some modification.

As was mentioned in the previous chapter, the Greek word for body is *soma*. The word for soul is *psyche* (psoo-KAY). From *psyche* is derived such English words as psychology, psychiatrist, and psychic, while *soma* and *psyche* are combined in the word "psychosomatic." However, *sarx*, "flesh," is distinct from either of these; yet, in a sense, it is a combination of both. *Sarx* refers to the physical and emotional elements of human life that are experienced in both body and mind.

As we have already noted, *sarx* is normally a rather neutral term. During the intertestimonial period, however, the concept of "flesh" became identified as the source of all sorts of passions that can be controlled only through the thorough-going application of "devout reason." This idea is illustrated in the wording of 4 Maccabees 7:17–18:

> Some perhaps might say, "Not all have full command of their emotions, because not all have prudent reason." But as many as attend to religion with a whole heart, these alone are able to control the passions of the flesh....

Paul often used "flesh" (*sarx*) in this same way, to denote destructive emotions that take control of a person:

> While we were living in the flesh, our sinful passions, aroused by the law, were at work in our members to bear fruit for death.
>
> Romans 7:5

> ...let us live honorably as in the day, not in reveling and drunkenness, not in debauchery and licentiousness, not in quarreling and jealousy. Instead, put on the Lord Jesus Christ, and make no provision for the flesh, to gratify its desires.
>
> Romans 13:13–14

Paul contrasted life in the flesh (*sarx*) with life in the spirit (*pneuma*) in two of his letters (Romans 8:1–17; Galatians 5:16–26), and he spoke of the flesh as "sinful."

"Flesh," in Paul's view, embodies much that is destructive and alienating, including—but in no way limited to—sexual lust and license. Thus in Paul's writings "flesh" became transformed from a neutral term to one denoting an evil attitude that produces all sorts of societal ills:

> Now the works of the flesh are obvious: fornication, impurity, licentiousness, idolatry, sorcery, enmities, strife, jealousy, anger, quarrels, dissensions, factions, envy, drunkenness, carousing, and things like these. I am warning you, as I warned you before: those who do such things will not inherit the kingdom of God.

By contrast, the fruit of the Spirit is love, joy, peace, patience, kindness, generosity, faithfulness, gentleness, and self-control. There is no law against such things. And those who belong to Christ Jesus have crucified the flesh with its passions and desires.

Galatians 5:19–24

At one point Paul used *flesh* (*sarx*) as a synonym for *body* (*soma*):

Do you not know that whoever is united to a prostitute becomes one body with her? For it is said, "The two shall be one flesh."

1 Corinthians 6:16

Nonetheless, when Paul referred to married persons becoming "one flesh," *sarx* no longer meant the source of destructive passions. Instead, Paul spoke of "one flesh" in a positive and joyous manner.

Just as Jesus used the phrase "one flesh" as a basis for his ideal of marriage, so Paul used the same phrase as a basis for his teachings about both marriage and sexual morality. In doing so, Paul employed the word "flesh" in two ways, referring to one's physical body and to one's personality (although the two are always regarded as interactive).

"Flesh" as body

Let us first explore the way that Paul applied the phrase "one flesh" to a person's physical body.

Paul regarded sexual intercourse as a sign and symbol of two persons becoming "one flesh." By doing so, he imbued sexual intimacy with a surprising richness of meaning and value, to the point that his teachings may seem disturbingly alien to our own age. The central passage in which Paul expresses this thought is found in 1 Corinthians 6:15–20:

Do you not know that your bodies are members of Christ? Should I therefore take the members of Christ and make them members of a prostitute? Never! Do you not know that whoever is united to a prostitute becomes one body with her? For it is said, "The two shall be one flesh." But anyone united to the Lord becomes one spirit with him. Shun fornication! Every sin that a person commits is outside the body; but the fornicator sins against the body itself. Or do you not know that your body is a temple of the Holy Spirit within you, which you have from God, and that you are not your own? For you were bought with a price; therefore glorify God in your body.

Paul's reasoning in this passage may puzzle modern readers. Moreover, his wording is too concise, with one thought tersely expressed and then suddenly giving way to a different thought. Paul probably used this brisk writing style because he was simply reminding his readers of things that he had already taught them more extensively when he was with them. His statements, then, are simply flags referring to longer, more carefully argued teachings that the Corinthian Christians had already heard and affirmed.

Modern readers, therefore, will find it difficult to understand Paul's discourse. We are forced to engage in the somewhat subjective task of trying to flesh out the apostle's reasoning and fill in the transitions.

Let us begin by remembering that this letter was addressed to a church located in Corinth, a city that provided prostitution as a major product. High above this city, atop a stone monolith, stood a huge temple to Aphrodite, goddess of fertility. This temple boasted that it owned one thousand prostitutes, reported a Greek traveler named Herodotus, who added that not every sailor could afford to visit Corinth!

So when Paul told these new Christians that they were not to be united with a prostitute, they listened. When Paul said that they were not to engage in fornication (that is, sexual intimacy with anyone except one's marriage partner), they understood.

Behind Paul's instructions we can glimpse three affirmations. First, underlying Paul's reasoning is the belief that sexuality is God's creation and therefore is good. Our bodies belong to God.[1]

Therefore, we are given stewardship of our bodies, lest they be misused. Moreover, our bodies, as gifts from God, are to be a means by which we glorify God (verse 20).

So we are to exercise sexual restraint, his teachings imply, not because sex is bad, but precisely because it is good. Sex is a "gift" of God (1 Corinthians 7:7). Marriage may even lead to the salvation of an unbelieving partner as well as the salvation of children born of such a union (7:14–16).

Because sex (in marriage) is good, a couple should not abstain for any great length of time. The Jewish schools of Shammai and Hillel disagreed over how long a man might abstain—either two weeks (Shammai), or one week (Hillel) and then only if his wife agrees.[2] In a similar manner Paul argued that such a period of abstinence be short and that a couple abstain only for the purpose of prayer (7:5–6).

Second, Paul spoke of sexual intimacy as the union of two persons. Paul used a spiritual analogy to plead his case. When a person unites with the Lord, Paul wrote, he or she becomes one spirit with the Lord. Similarly, in sexual intercourse a person becomes one flesh with his or her partner. Paul's words imply that if a person regards sexual intercourse as simply recreation or a means of gratification, that person has betrayed the nature and value of sex. He or she is simply using his or her sex partner as a means of masturbation.

On the other hand, Paul did not regard sexual intercourse as solely a means of procreation.

Sexual intercourse, according to Paul, is far more than a mere physical act. It is intended to represent the union of two beings. It is also meant to be a means of praising the Creator of the human body. One's body is a temple, in which one glorifies God (1 Corinthans 6:19–20). In that sense, sex is worship.

Third, behind Paul's words lies the conviction that what we do with our bodies effects us mentally and spiritually. We cannot separate the physical from the spiritual. Our bodies are members of Christ, he writes (6:15), "therefore, glorify God in your body"(6:20).

Paul included a remarkable statement about our bodies when he wrote, "your body is a temple" (6:19). That statement too implies that our bodies are good; it also implies that one's body is not an object of worship, but a means of worship. We are not to serve our bodies, but to serve God with our bodies.

This metaphor must have startled many Greek thinkers, who regarded the physical body as a prison of the spirit. One's body pulls one around with its passions, they argued. Many other Greeks believed that one's spirit and one's body are separate and distinct, so that what we do with the one has little effect upon the other.[3]

Not so for Paul! His call to "glorify God in your body" affirms the goodness of our physical selves in spiritual service to God.

Basing his sense of sexual morality on these three principles, Paul gave specific instructions to his readers regarding sexual behavior. Engaging a prostitute violates the very meaning and nature of sex. So do adultery and fornication, because they too run counter to the divine origin and purpose of sex. Sexual intercourse is intended to be both a means of affirming the becoming of "one flesh" with one's partner and of glorifying God in one's body.

If we extend Paul's thought, then, we will define a sexual sin as any violation of the intended purpose and nature of one's sexuality: to affirm a marriage covenant and to glorify God.

From this basis Paul developed a high code of sexual morality. Our bodies belong to Christ (1 Corinthians 6:15), he declared; therefore, as Christians we are to avoid fornication, impurity, and licentiousness (Galatians 5:19) and pursue a quality of life that produces the fruit of the Spirit—"love, joy, peace, patience, kindness, generosity, faithfulness, gentleness, and self-control" (Galatians 5:22–26).

"Flesh" as more than body

In spite of Paul's lofty regard for the sanctity of marital sex, he argued that celibacy is better than marriage for two reasons.

First, it would be better for Christians not to marry, he wrote, because of the "impending crisis." By this, he was probably referring either to the difficulty and risk of being a Christian or else to the expected return of Christ (1 Corinthians 7:25–31).

Second, it would be better for a Christian to remain single because a married person is divided between wanting to serve the Lord and wanting to please his or her partner (1 Corinthians 7:32–35):

> I want you to be free from anxieties. The unmarried man is anxious about the affairs of the Lord, how to please the Lord; but the married man is anxious about the affairs of the world, how to please his wife, and his interests are divided. And the unmarried woman and the virgin are anxious about the affairs of the Lord, so that they may be holy in body and spirit; but the married woman is anxious about the affairs of the world, how to please her husband. I say this for your own benefit, not to put any restraint upon you, but to promote good order and unhindered devotion to the Lord.

Although searching for a way to spare Christians from that kind of conflict, Paul never once suggested that the quality of the marriage relationship should be compromised. He did not ask married Christians to separate; instead, he urged them to be attentive to the needs and desires of their marriage partners. Being "one flesh" involves a deep caring for one's mate that is not to be reduced by one's commitment to Christ.

However, in the case where a believer is married to an unbeliever and the unbeliever prefers divorce, Paul readily concurs:

> To the married I give this command—not I but the Lord— that the wife should not separate from her husband (but if she does separate, let her remain unmarried or else be reconciled to her husband), and that the husband should not divorce his wife. To the rest I say—I and not the Lord—that if any believer has a wife who is an unbeliever, and she consents to live with him, he should not divorce her. And if any woman has a husband who is an unbeliever, and he consents

to live with her, she should not divorce him. For the unbelieving husband is made holy through his wife, and the unbelieving wife is made holy through her husband. Otherwise, your children would be unclean, but as it is, they are
holy. But if the unbelieving partner separates, let it be so; in
such a case the brother or sister is not bound. It is to peace
that God has called you. Wife, for all you know, you might
save your husband. Husband, for all you know, you might
save your wife.

1 Corinthians 7:10–16

In Paul's view, being one spirit with Christ takes precedence
over being one flesh with an unbelieving marriage partner.

The author of Ephesians (many scholars have concluded
that it was not Paul) continued the theme of "one flesh" in three
remarkable ways.

First, he used military terms to describe a married couple
(Ephesians 5:22–24):

Wives, be subject to your husbands as you are to the Lord.
For the husband is the head of the wife just as Christ is the
head of the church, the body of which he is the Savior. Just as
the church is subject to Christ, so also wives ought to be, in
everything, to their husbands.

The translation of this passage is inadequate, in that two
key words in Greek are military terms. The husband, the writer
argued, is the "head" of the wife. The word translated "head,"
kephale (kef-ah-LAY), denotes the "point man" in a phalanx.
The wife, the writer went on to say, is to "be subject to" her
husband. The word translated "be subject to," *hupotassomai* (hoo-
poh-TASS-oh-my), when applied to soldiers means to stand in
formation with one's comrades.[4]

In this military analogy, husband and wife serve together,
both following the same orders of the same commander, each
depending upon the support and cooperation of the other. This
word picture was so contrary to marriage practices among Jews
and pagans alike that its implication was soon lost within the
church.

Second, the writer suggested that the relationship between Christ and his church represents an ideal model for marriage (Ephesians 5:25–32):

> Husbands, love your wives, just as Christ loved the church and gave himself up for her, in order to make her holy by cleansing her with the washing of water by the word, so as to present the church to himself in splendor, without a spot or wrinkle or anything of the kind—yes, so that she may be holy and without blemish. In the same way, husbands should love their wives as they do their own bodies. He who loves his wife loves himself. For no one ever hates his own body, but he nourishes and tenderly cares for it, just as Christ does for the church, because we are members of his body. "For this reason a man will leave his father and mother and be joined to his wife, and the two will become one flesh." This is a great mystery, and I am applying it to Christ and the church.

Just as Christ willingly gave his life for his church and now nourishes his church and cares for it, so a husband is to love his wife with the same kind of intense devotion.

Making the husband analogous to Christ has alienated many modern readers from this passage. People living during the early centuries of the church's life, however, would have found these words disturbing for a different reason. Greek philosophy taught that a man was to rule over his wife as a master over a servant or as one's rational mind over one's emotions. The author of Ephesians challenged this by proposing that husbands imitate the kind of leadership qualities that Christ demonstrated: humble service and ultimate self-giving. This argument was so radical that its thrust was usually disregarded in the writings and preaching of the church fathers. In its place they advocated a hierarchical model for marriage, in which a husband wields benevolent authority over his wife.

Third, the author of Ephesians wrote of a unity between a married couple that is compared to the unity of a man with his own body (5:28–30): "In the same way, husbands should love their wives as they do their own bodies. He who loves his wife

loves himself" (verse 28). This passage has been misused to justify a condescending attitude on the part of husbands toward
their wives, inviting a comparison of the masculine with rational mind and the feminine with fleshly passion. However, the
words were written in opposition to that very attitude. "He who
loves his wife loves himself" (verse 28b) implies that a man cannot put his wife down without also putting himself down.

The wording has been further misused to justify physical
and sexual abuse within marriage. Some men have twisted the
wording in this verse to give themselves authority to do what
they wish with their wives' bodies. Such an interpretation is
possible only if one deliberately disregards the meaning of the
word *love*.

Summary

Because the church proclaimed a high code of sexual morality accompanied by a special value placed upon celibacy, two
distortions have resulted.

First, Paul's teachings about sexual immorality were sepa-
rated out from his teaching about other forms of sin. Sins of the
body became distinct from other sins of the flesh (greed, lying,
and so forth), to the point that the phrase "sins of the flesh"
became almost synonymous with sexual immorality.

Second, the affirmation that we are saved only by grace was
dimmed by a strong appeal for Christians to achieve holiness
through the denial of natural desires and passions.

Both Jesus and Paul taught a high ethic, but it was always
accompanied by an even greater sense of God's grace. Jesus' call
for sexual purity far outstripped that of his contemporaries, yet
Jesus could forgive an adulterous woman whom others would
have stoned to death. Advocating the ideal of "one flesh" automatically increased both opportunity for failure and, with it,
the need for grace.

Too often the church has reiterated Paul's distinction between law and grace in all matters except those pertaining to
sexuality and marriage.

Notes

[1]Note how Paul often linked sexual immorality with greediness and envy, as in 1 Corinthians 5:11; 6:9–10; Galatians 5:19–21.

[2]*m. Ketub.* 5:6.

[3]Certainly this idea was not shared by everyone who had been schooled in Greek philosophy; however, it was a major tenet within the various viewpoints collectively referred to as "Gnostic."

[4]For a fuller discussion of these words, see my book, *What Paul Really Said About Women* (San Francisco: Harper, 1988).

Questions for Discussion

1. In this chapter, the claim is made that Paul regarded sex as God's good gift. How would this idea be received by one who has suffered sexual abuse?

2. To what extent is the idea that sexual intercourse involves the union of two persons incompatible with the attitudes and practices within our society after the sexual revolution?

3. Paul's teachings imply that what we do with our bodies effects us spiritually. If that is true, what does it say about the relationship of worship and work?

4. The doctrine of encratism arose from an attitude that regarded sexual intimacy as somehow sinful. Is that attitude still expressed by some Christian groups today? If so, in what ways?

5. Should churches teach matters pertaining to sexuality and sexual intimacy? If so, to what ages and in what manner?

8

Divorce in the Teachings of Jesus

One time some Pharisees came to Jesus and asked him a question: "Is it lawful for a man to divorce his wife for any cause?" Jesus' reply was so radical that even his own disciples objected to it.

Because the topic is so important and Jesus' words are so easily misunderstood, it is helpful to examine closely the way both Matthew and Mark report the incident (Luke does not include it):

> Some Pharisees came to him, and to test him they asked, "Is it lawful for a man to divorce his wife for any cause?" He

103

answered, "Have you not read that the one who made them at the beginning 'made them male and female,' and said, 'For this reason a man shall leave his father and mother and be joined to his wife, and the two shall become one flesh'? So they are no longer two, but one flesh. Therefore what God has joined together, let no one separate." They said to him, "Why then did Moses command us to give a certificate of dismissal and to divorce her?" He said to them, "It was because you were so hard-hearted that Moses allowed you to divorce your wives, but from the beginning it was not so. And I say to you, whoever divorces his wife, except for unchastity, and marries another commits adultery."* His disciples said to him, "If such is the case of a man with his wife, it is better not to marry." But he said to them, "Not everyone can accept this teaching, but only those to whom it is given."

Matthew 19:3–11

Some Pharisees came, and to test him they asked, "Is it lawful for a man to divorce his wife?" He answered them, "What did Moses command you?" They said, "Moses allowed a man to write a certificate of dismissal and to divorce her." But Jesus said to them, "Because of your hardness of heart he wrote this commandment for you. But from the beginning of creation, 'God made them male and female.' 'For this reason a man shall leave his father and mother and be joined to his wife, and the two shall become one flesh.' So they are no longer two, but one flesh. Therefore what God has joined together, let no one separate."

Then in the house the disciples asked him again about this matter. He said to them, "Whoever divorces his wife and marries another commits adultery against her; and if she divorces her husband and marries another, she commits adultery."

Mark 10:2–12

---

*Other ancient authorities read *except on the grounds of unchastity, causes her to commit adultery;* others add at the end of the verse *and he who marries a divorced woman commits adultery.*

A question of law

In order to understand the question that the Pharisees asked Jesus, we need to understand its legal background. The only "law" regarding divorce is found in Deuteronomy 24:1–4:

> Suppose a man enters into marriage with a woman, but she does not please him because he finds something objectionable about her, and so he writes her a certificate of divorce, puts it in her hand, and sends her out of his house; she then leaves his house and goes off to become another man's wife. Then suppose the second man dislikes her, writes her a bill of divorce, puts it in her hand, and sends her out of his house (or the second man who married her dies); her first husband, who sent her away, is not permitted to take her again to be his wife after she has been defiled; for that would be abhorrent to the LORD, and you shall not bring guilt on the land that the LORD your God is giving you as a possession.

In reality, this passage in and of itself is not a law about divorce. It sets up a situation in order to present a law that has to do with remarrying one's ex-wife. Since there are no specific divorce laws in the Old Testament, however, this passage became the basis for rules about divorce within Judean society.

The wording in this statute concerning divorce itself, however, is very vague. A man, according to this passage, may divorce his wife if "he finds something objectionable about her." That is not specific enough to be very helpful in establishing what is and what is not a just cause for divorce. All it says is that a man can divorce his wife if he is displeased with her—implying, at best, that a man cannot divorce his wife if he is *not* displeased with her! So the scribes (the students of the God's *torah*, the law) tried to determine the intention behind that phrase, "something objectionable" (Hebrew *'erwat dabar*).

There were two schools of thought on that issue in Jesus' day. According to Rabbi Shammai, the only "objectionable" behavior that justified divorce was adultery. A man might divorce his wife only if she were unfaithful to him. According to Rabbi Hillel, however, "something objectionable" could include all manner of things, such as her being childless, insulting her husband's parents, or even putting too much salt in his food. (Guess which of these two schools of thought was most popular among the men!)

As a result, many men acted as if their marriages were disposable. The divorce rate was so high in the time of Jesus that a significant number of young women simply refused to get married.

So when the Pharisees asked Jesus, "Is it lawful for a man to divorce his wife for any cause?" they were dealing with a burning contemporary social issue.

Only husbands could divorce wives

Notice that in the law of Moses divorce could be initiated only by the husband. The possibility that a man's wife might find displeasure in him and wish to divorce him was not even considered. This one-sided view of the matter originates with the attitude that regarded women as sexual property. Women could not initiate divorce, because they were their husbands' property. In fact, a woman was expected to address her spouse with the phrase *be'ulat ba'al,* "lord husband."

In Chapter 1 we noted that this principle of sexual property led to some rather curious laws in the Old Testament (from a modern viewpoint, anyway). A woman's father or her husband had the right to annul a vow that she had made to God (Numbers 30:3–5). Rape was a crime not against the woman, but against her father (Exodus 22:16–17). A maiden's loss of virginity was regarded, not so much as sin, but as property damage, for which her father was to be compensated (Exodus 22:16–17).

Most important for our understanding of Jesus' response to the Pharisees' question about divorce, however, is this: the principle of sexual property meant that although a married woman could commit adultery against her husband, a husband could not commit adultery against his wife. As noted earlier, if a married man had sexual relations with an unmarried woman, it was not adultery. After all, he was not his wife's sexual property. Only if he had sexual relations with a married woman was it regarded as adultery. Adultery was never a sin against the man's own wife, but against the other woman's husband!

It is remarkable, then, that in Mark's account Jesus added the words, "and if she divorces her husband and marries another, she commits adultery" (Mark 10:12). Many scholars have concluded that these words were added because Mark's Gospel was written in Rome, and Roman women were permitted to initiate divorce. In other words, the evangelist, according to this suggestion, simply accommodated Jesus' teachings to the prevailing social milieu in order to avoid having this scripture apply only to men.[1]

However, since Jesus often demonstrated great respect for women and rejected the double standard within his society, it may be that Mark's Gospel is faithfully recording Jesus' intention—and perhaps even his specific teaching.

The notion that women are sexual property, combined with a sense of the sacred authority of Deuteronomy 24:1–2, constituted the social and legal background to the question about divorce. The question that the Pharisees posed to Jesus was simply this: under what conditions might a man legally divest himself of his sexual property? Unless we understand the nature and background of their inquiry, we will fail to appreciate Jesus' answer.

Jesus responded by addressing the legal aspect of the issue, the prevalent attitudes about marriage, and the effect of divorce upon Judean women.

A matter of law

Jesus carefully distinguished between the words of Moses and the words of God. In referring to Deuteronomy 24:1–2, Jesus said, "It was because you were so hard-hearted that Moses allowed you to divorce your wives, but from the beginning it was not so" (Matthew 19:8). It was not God who allowed men to dismiss their wives, it was Moses. This is communicated even more clearly in Mark's version: "Because of your hardness of heart he [Moses] wrote this commandment for you" (Mark 10:5).

Jesus' words challenge the notion that every portion of the scriptures came from God. We often refer to the Bible as "the word of God," but Christ's statement indicates that he did not believe that every biblical passage has a divine origin.[2]

After making a distinction between the law of Moses from the will of God, Jesus then challenged the law of Moses by declaring that "whoever divorces his wife and marries another commits adultery against her" (Mark 10:11).

This was an extremely radical position, since according to the law it was not even possible for a man to commit adultery against his own wife! For Jesus, however, marriage was not simply the legal ownership of a sexual possession. It was a physical and spiritual relationship between two persons. The law might permit what in reality violates the very nature of that relationship.

By his response Jesus declared that something may be legal and yet not be just. The law may permit a man to put his wife out of their home, but that action does not in and of itself sever their marriage bond. A man may have the legal right to marry a woman who has been dismissed by her formal husband, but that does not mean that her relationship with her first husband is thereby dissolved.

Attitudes about women

Jesus' answer went beyond the question of legality. He challenged the attitudes about marriage reflected in his culture in three ways:

First, he rejected the prevalent attitude that regarded women as sex objects rather than persons. We have identified several instances when he challenged that notion. (See Chapter 5.)

Jesus declared that a man who lusts after a woman (that is, desires to have her as his sexual possession) thereby commits adultery with her in his heart. In order to understand this text, we must remember that people in biblical times believed that the *heart* was the center of human thoughts. Wherever the scripture writers used *heart*, today we would use the word *mind*. Therefore, when Jesus spoke of "hardness of heart," we would say "narrow-minded" or something similar.

The Gospel of Luke reports an incident when a woman of ill repute came up to Jesus during a dinner party and began to wash his feet (Luke 7:36–50). The host regarded the woman only in terms of her immoral sexual history. Jesus, on the other hand, responded to her as a person. He spoke to her directly, he referred to her actions, her love, her sins, and her faith.

Jesus affirmed women as persons in many other instances. In Samaria he met with a woman who had been married five times and now was living with a man to whom she was not married. Instead of condemning her, Jesus instead spoke to her about spiritual thirst and about his own ability to satisfy that deep need. Later Jesus welcomed those to whom she had witnessed (John 4:1–42).

Jesus personally engaged in what many regarded as "women's work," such as washing other's feet and preparing food (John 13:1–11; 21:9–10).

Jesus refused to regard bearing children as a woman's highest calling. One time a woman in the crowd said of Jesus' mother, "Blessed is the womb that bore you and the breasts that nursed you!" But Jesus said, "Blessed rather are those who hear the word of God and obey it!" (Luke 11:27–28).

Jesus included women among his band of disciples (Mark 15:40–41), he taught women such as Mary and Martha (Luke 10:38–42), and he commissioned certain women to proclaim his resurrection (a fact reported by all four Gospel writers).

In these and other ways Jesus demonstrated his rejection of the attitude that regarded women as sexual possessions.

Attitudes about marriage

Second, Jesus distanced himself from the law of Moses on the matter of attitudes toward marriage itself.

Note Jesus' use of pronouns. He did not speak of Moses' law as applying to "us"; instead, he spoke of how Moses commanded "you" or "allowed you" (Mark 10:3; Matthew 19:8). He stated that Moses gave this law because of "your hardness of heart"(Mark 10:5). Jesus placed this law squarely in the context of an attitude that he himself did not share.

Moreover, Jesus contrasted God's will with Moses' law. What Moses allowed, Jesus insisted, was not justice but compromise. God's intention from the beginning of creation, however, was that a man and woman become "one flesh."

Marriage as a covenant

Third, Jesus was not so concerned with when a marriage can end as how a marriage can succeed. The men of his day might assuage their consciences by giving their wives certificates of divorce (rather than simply kicking them out of their homes), but Jesus reminded them what marriage was meant to be in "the beginning" (Matthew 19:8; Mark 10:6).

As we saw in Chapter 5, Jesus based his teachings about marriage on the companionship model, found in the relationship of Adam and Eve before the fall. Jesus claimed that it is God's intention that a couple be "one flesh." In other words, a husband and wife are to become like parts of the same body, sensing each other's pain and joy as if these feelings were their own and caring for each other as much as they care for themselves. A successful marriage is not just one in which the wife pleases the husband, but one in which both please each other.

The words used by God to describe the relationship of Eve to Adam (see Chapter 4) portray the couple as equals. Therefore, according to Genesis 2, marriage was not intended to be the relationship of a man and his sexual possession, but of two people who share each other's desires and hopes and who mutually decide on the pattern and direction of their life together.

More than that, it was God's intention that a man "leave" his parents and be "joined" (or "cling") to his wife (Genesis 2:24; Matthew 19:5). Both of these words were often used in the Bible to describe the forming of a covenant, a bond of agreement. The word translated "leave" is used elsewhere for when a person leaves off worshiping idols to worship the living God. The word translated "be joined" is used elsewhere for when a person enters into a solemn and lasting relationship with God.

Jesus' argument challenged prevailing attitudes and practices at this crucial point: marriage is designed by God to be a covenant between two persons. If so, then the success of a marriage is never simply a question of whether the wife pleases her husband, precisely because it takes two to make a marriage work. It is a covenant; therefore, it depends upon both parties.

Judean marriage practices

Judean divorce practices were particularly unfair to wives. A woman who was divorced had only four options: she might live for some time on her dowry (providing that her husband had not managed to keep it, something that was often permitted); she might return to her parents' home (if they were still living and were able to take her in) or live with some other relatives (if they would receive her); she might hope for and seek out a new husband (difficult for a woman to do in that culture); or, she might support herself through prostitution.

Jesus' response to the Pharisees' question pointedly addressed the difficulties faced by divorced women in that time and in that culture. If a man chose to divorce his wife in order to marry another woman, Jesus' teachings imply, his actions may have been legal, but they also may have been unjust and cruel. This fact is reflected in Jesus' unusual wording about divorce earlier in the Sermon on the Mount (Matthew 5:31–32):

> It was also said, "Whoever divorces his wife, let him give her a certificate of divorce." But I say to you that anyone who divorces his wife, except on the ground of unchastity, causes her to commit adultery; and whoever marries a divorced woman commits adultery.

Note carefully his wording: "anyone who divorces his wife, except on the grounds of unchastity, *causes her to commit adul-*

tery" (italics added). Some of the ancient New Testament manuscripts repeated those very same words later, in Jesus' response to the Pharisees' question about divorce (Matthew 19:9): "whoever divorces his wife, except on the ground of unchastity, and marries another causes her to commit adultery" (alternative reading).

If this is the original reading, then Jesus was saying something like this: "Husband, when you divorce your wife she may be left with only two options, to marry another man or else to become a prostitute. Either way, you have forced her to have sexual relations with another man. What you are doing may be legal, but it forces your wife to commit adultery."

In other manuscripts, however, Jesus' words in this verse read differently: "whoever divorces his wife, except for unchastity, and marries another commits adultery." If this is the original reading, then Jesus was saying something like this: "Husband, it may be legal for you to dismiss your wife, but it is nonetheless immoral. According to the law, you are not committing adultery, but it hurts your wife just as much."

Shocked disciples

Jesus' position on marriage and divorce was unpopular, even among his own disciples (Matthew 19:10; compare Mark 10:10). Jesus admitted that his teaching was not for everyone, but only for those who were able: "Not everyone can accept this teaching, but only those to whom it is given" (Matthew 19:11).

In subsequent centuries, however, numerous Christians have taken the words of Jesus about divorce and marriage very literally and very seriously, insisting that a Christian should not divorce, cannot remarry, and would do better by not getting married in the first place. As a result, celibacy became a qualification for true holiness, churches passed laws forbidding divorce, and pious folk have often done their best to make people who are suffering from bad marriages feel even worse.

How then can we today regard this passage of scripture? Are we to outlaw divorce? Are we to condemn those who are already hurting from a bad marriage? Are we to say, along with Jesus' disciples, "If such is the case of a man with his wife, it is better not to marry" (Matthew 19:10)? Did Jesus intend for his followers to do this? If not, what did he intend?

To make Jesus' words about divorce into a new legal code would violate his intent and his example. Because Jesus rejected the model of marriage as a legal contract, we as his followers dare not represent his words as a new or revised law. Instead, let's remember that Jesus was reminding his followers of the original goal of marriage. He lifted up the model of "one flesh" as the ideal model for marriage.

However, the very act of presenting an ideal automatically creates an even greater possibility for failure. Any ideal will become an oppressive source of discouragement unless we exercise an even greater amount of grace and mercy.

We need to hold onto the ideal, but let us also remember that Christ always placed grace above the ideal. He expanded the definition of adultery, for example, but he also forgave the woman caught in adultery (John 8:1–11). We are to strive toward a goal, yes, yet we are forgiven when we fail—so that we may pick ourselves up and try again. After all, if God's grace is sufficient when we fail in other areas of life, is it not also sufficient when we fail to achieve marital success?

Notes

[1] The Jewish Talmud, a collection of interpretations and applications of the Mosaic law that was compiled almost two centuries after Christ, does allow wives to divorce their husbands in certain circumstances, such as in the event that the husband works as a tanner (in handling dead animals every day, a tanner was apt to become ritually "unclean"). It may be that some wives were allowed to divorce their husbands in Judean society at the time of Christ, which could account for the wording in Mark's account.

[2] However, in Mark 7:10–13 Jesus does equate certain words of Moses with "the word of God."

Questions for Discussion

1. Because modern laws regarding divorce differ from those in first-century Judea, do Jesus' words have any relevance for our divorce laws today? If so, in what ways?

2. Since our culture has been moving away from the attitude that regards women as the sexual property of men, how do Jesus' words and actions affirming women as persons relate to our society?

3. Because women in our society have opportunities to earn money and because divorce laws provide for child support from fathers, do Jesus' words about "causing her to commit adultery" have any meaning for us today?

4. How do churches present the teachings of Jesus regarding divorce? How should they?

5. Is it possible to advocate a high ideal regarding marriage and yet regard instances of marital failure with a sense of grace?

9

Christ's Rejection
of Family Loyalty

The scriptures do not extol the virtues of family life to the extent that most readers might expect. The first book in the Bible begins with a family (one of the few examples of a nuclear family in the Bible) in which one son murders the other (Genesis 4:1–16), and the last of the pastoral epistles in the New Testament recommends that young mothers should be taught to love their children (Titus 2:4). Instead of painting an idyllic picture of family life, the scriptures honestly portray those difficulties and risks that parents often encounter.

Family patterns in ancient Israel

In the Old Testament world, the word *family* meant something quite different than it does for us today. Israelites were divided into tribes, tribes divided into clans, and clans divided into families. A family was usually referred to as one's *bet-'ab*, one's father's *house* (*household* in the NRSV). A household was composed of the patriarch and his wife or wives (or concubines), his sons and their wives, his grandsons and their wives, plus any unmarried sons or daughters of any generation below him, as well as an assortment of servants. A typical *bet-'ab* would have comprised somewhere between fifty and a hundred individuals (including all nonrelated dependents), living together in a cluster of residences.

Achan, for example, was married and had children, but he was part of house of Zabdi, his great-grandfather (Joshua 7:18). Likewise, Gideon, who was married and had at least one son (Judges 8:20) and servants (Judges 6:27), was under the authority of his father Joash (Judges 6:30).

Each *bet-'ab* had its own land inheritance. Great efforts were made to keep this property within the family. If use of the land was sold, the family was guaranteed the option of redeeming it (Leviticus 25:23–24):

> The land shall not be sold in perpetuity, for the land is mine; with me you are but aliens and tenants. Throughout the land that you hold, you shall provide for the redemption of the land.

If one generation within a family was forced to sell its land and could not redeem it, the property nonetheless would be transferred back to the family during Jubilee, a time every fiftieth year when land that had changed hands within the clan was returned to its original *bet-'ab*.

Patriarchal family structure

In Chapter 3 we read the story of how Rebekah conspired with her son Jacob to deceive her husband, Isaac. The goal of their fraudulent behavior was to trick Isaac into bestowing the patriarchal blessing upon Jacob rather than upon Jacob's firstborn twin brother, Esau. From our modern point of view the whole thing may seem rather trivial. So what if Isaac blessed Jacob instead of Esau? Is that a criminal offense?

Yes. At least in that culture in that age such a deception would be as serious as stuffing the ballot box at a corporation's board meeting in modern times.

Israelite families were ruled over by the eldest male, the *roshbet-'ab* (literally, "head of the father's house"). Remember that this patriarch acted for the family similar to the way a chief executive officer does for a corporation in our own society. The *rosh-bet-'ab* would represent his family, structure it, defend it, and oversee its productivity.

When the patriarch grew too old to perform these tasks, he would then bestow his position, power, and prestige upon his firstborn son. He did so by laying his hands upon his eldest son's head and pronouncing a blessing over him. This verbal blessing had all the force of a modern written contract. Through it, the firstborn son became the new patriarch.

The survival of a patriarchal family, then, depended upon a couple giving birth to at least one son who would outlive his father. However, the more children a couple might produce, the better off they would be. After all, children were the only means of security for one's old age. Therefore the psalmist equated having children with being blessed by God.

> Happy is everyone who fears the LORD,
>   who walks in his ways.
> You shall eat the fruit of the labor of your hands;
>   you shall be happy, and it shall go well with you.
> Your wife will be like a fruitful vine
>   within your house;
> your children will be like olive shoots
>   around your table.
> Thus shall the man be blessed
>   who fears the LORD.

The LORD bless you from Zion.
> May you see the prosperity of Jerusalem
> all the days of your life.
May you see your children's children.
> Peace be upon Israel!

Psalm 128

Need for children

It was not simple paternal or maternal sentiments that equated children with God's blessings:

> I will look with favor upon you and make you fruitful and multiply you; and I will maintain my covenant with you.

Leviticus 26:9

> Blessed shall be the fruit of your womb, the fruit of your ground, and the fruit of your livestock, both the increase of your cattle and the issue of your flock.

Deuteronomy 28:4

People in biblical times had no social security, no pension plans, no Medicare. An elderly couple's lives and well-being depended upon their adult children (especially their sons). These sons would provide them with food, clothing, health care, and defense against physical attacks from enemies. When the psalmist sang that sons are like arrows in a man's quiver (Psalm 127:3–5a), the truth behind that statement was more literal than modern readers might suppose:

> Sons are indeed a heritage from the LORD,
> > the fruit of the womb a reward.
> Like arrows in the hand of a warrior
> > are the sons of one's youth.
> Happy is the man
> > who has his quiver full of them.

If having children was a blessing in ancient Hebrew society, then barrenness was regarded as a grave misfortune, precisely because children were necessary in order for aged parents to survive. A lack of children could even be viewed as God's curse upon a woman, one in which "the LORD had closed up her womb" (1 Samuel 1:5; compare Genesis 30:2).

Having children was so important in ancient Israel that if a young married man died without producing a son, his wife would be given to the deceased man's brother in order that he might provide the widow with a son, who would then inherit the deceased man's property (the custom known as levirate marriage—see Chapter 2).

The sin of Onan, who was ordered into a levirate marriage with his widowed sister-in-law Tamar, was not simply that he "spilled his semen on the ground." His offense was practicing birth control within the patriarchal system. Keeping the patriarchal system intact was so important that Tamar's outrageous action of playing the part of a prostitute to her father-in-law was regarded as righteous.

Within the patriarchal system children were regarded as the property of their parents, the "fruit of the womb" (Deuteronomy 28:4; Isaiah 13:18). This ownership by parents was almost without limit. A father might sell his daughter into concubinage (Exodus 21:7–11) or his children into slavery as working pledges against loans (compare Nehemiah 5:1–5 and 2 Kings 4:1–7). Moreover, Israelite parents were even allowed to call for the death penalty upon their sons (Deuteronomy 21:18–21):

> If someone has a stubborn and rebellious son who will not obey his father and mother, who does not heed them when they discipline him, then his father and his mother shall take hold of him and bring him out to the elders of his town at the gate of that place. They shall say to the elders of his town, "This son of ours is stubborn and rebellious. He will not obey us. He is a glutton and a drunkard." Then all the men of the town shall stone him to death. So you shall purge the evil from your midst; and all Israel will hear, and be afraid.[1]

This ownership of children, however, was not as extensive as the law of *patria potestas* among the Romans, in that an Israelite father did not have absolute control of the life and death over his children. According to the law in Deuteronomy, both parents had to agree to request the death penalty for their son, and even then the final decision was left to a court of elders. Moreover, this law required that both parents testify, even though in other matters a woman's testimony was not accepted in a court of law.

In addition, the laws of ancient Israel, unlike those of neighboring cultures, excluded a "child for a child" kind of retribution when one child was killed (Exodus 21:28–32; Exodus 21:22; Deuteronomy 24:16; compare 2 Kings 14:5–6).

The patriarchal system, however, promoted favoritism on the part of the father toward his eldest son. This inequality among siblings often incited jealousy and intrigue among sons and mothers, illustrated so well in the stories of Esau and Jacob, Joseph and his brothers, Solomon and Adonijah.

Moreover, the fact that having many children contributed to a couple's well-being encouraged overpopulation. An ancient Mesopotamian version of the flood (predating the story of Noah) tells that the gods decided to flood the earth because there were too many people and the noises made by humanity kept the deities awake at night.

Population levels were reduced from time to time by war, famine, pestilence, and wild beasts—the terrible four horses of the apocalypse (Revelation 6:1–8). However, within many Mediterranean cultures a religiously approved method of population control was exercised, that of child sacrifice. The Hebrews, however, were forbidden by their laws from offering children on the altar. The story of Abraham's aborted attempt to offer Isaac as a sacrifice may have been recorded in order to emphasize that prohibition. However, the Israelites did retain the idea of giving their children to God. Although Jewish parents were not allowed to slay their children on altars,[2] some dedicated their children to God and left them under the care of a priest, as Hannah did with her firstborn son, Samuel (1 Samuel 1:24–28).

Families of oppression

The greatest problem within the patriarchal system of ancient Israel was that some families grew very large and powerful at the expense of smaller families and individuals. Members of a large family would trade with one another, defend each other, and retain their wealth among their own kindred. All of this worked to the detriment of members of smaller families, even more so among widows and orphans.

The patriarchal system, therefore, became a source of oppression for many within Israel. Individuals who did not have family ties were regarded as nobodies. This is reflected in a dramatic way by that Old Testament law that says a bastard is to be excluded from the society of Israel, as are his descendants even to the tenth generation (Deuteronomy 23:3)!

In those days, "family values" meant preserving one's own family's wealth and power, often at the expense of those who lacked large numbers of kindred.

Jesus' family of origin

One such individual was Jesus of Nazareth. His parents, although marginally descendants of King David, were of humble stock, living in a small village in the hills of Galilee. Galileans were regarded as hotheaded hillbillies by the more urbanized citizens of Judea, who joked about how these northerners spoke with an accent and questioned whether Galileans were really Jews at all.

Moreover, Jesus' hometown was belittled, even by other Galileans. The Gospel of John (1:46) relat' at Nathanael (a resident of Bethsaida and therefore a Gali' elf) ridiculed Jesus' village by asking, "Can anyth' come out of Nazareth?" Although Nazareth was ly an hour's distance from the Roman metropoli ris, this proximity to a Gentile city would not have e status of Nazarenes in the eyes of faithful Jews.

Jesus was the eldest child by today's standards would be a large family, composed of ti sons (including Jesus) and at least two daughters:

> He came to his hometown and began to teach the people in
> their synagogue, so that they were astounded and said, "Where

did this man get this wisdom and these deeds of power? Is
not this the carpenter's son? Is not his mother called Mary?
And are not his brothers James and Joseph and Simon and
Judas? And are not all his sisters with us?"

Matthew 13:54–56a (compare Mark 6:3)

Jesus' position in his family should have given him some
meager amount of status, but the circumstances of his birth
apparently led some people to regard him as a bastard (John
8:41), and therefore not even a true Israelite (Deuteronomy
23:3). Besides, a peasant couple living in the hills of Galilee
would have very little wealth or prestige to bestow upon their
eldest son.

Although some of Jesus' contemporaries referred to him as
"the son of Joseph," no passage in the New Testament records
the fate of Joseph himself. The Gospel of Mark does not mention him at all. In Matthew, Joseph is associated only with the
infancy stories. In John, his name appears only as Jesus' father
(1:45; 6:42). In Luke, Joseph is present during one episode when
Jesus is twelve years old. Thereafter Joseph disappears from the
narration.

These omissions suggest that Joseph had already died before Jesus began his public ministry, leaving Mary in the role of
a single parent (this is supported by the way that the people of
Nazareth later refer to Jesus as "the son of Mary," Mark 6:3). If
so, Jesus may have waited to begin his ministry until he was
thirty (Luke 3:23) in order to remain at home and provide for
his family until his brothers and sisters were grown.

During his ministry, however, Jesus was certainly not close
to his family, nor did they affirm and encourage him. At one
point his family decided that he was mentally disturbed!

Then he went home; and the crowd came together again, so
that they could not even eat. When his family heard it, they
went out to restrain him, for people were saying, "He has
gone out of his mind."

Mark 3:19b–21

In spite of his successes, Jesus' own brothers did not believe in him (John 7:5). It was not until after Jesus' death and resurrection that one of them, James, became a believer and a leader in the church (Acts 1:14; 15:13–34; 21:18).

Therefore, Jesus' own family of origin was hardly an ideal model of family life! Given these glimpses into Jesus' background, we would probably be accurate in describing his boyhood family this way: large, poor, headed by a single mother, living in a village of negative repute situated within a remote district of a small country occupied by a foreign government (Rome).

If the reaction of Jesus' brothers is any indication of earlier sibling relationships, we might also classify Jesus' family of origin as dysfunctional. It is little wonder, then, that the people of Nazareth were astonished at Jesus' wisdom and effective power. They knew his background and his family members and asked with surprise, "Where then did this man get all this?" (Matthew 13:56).

One time Jesus' mother and brothers came to visit him, but he did not welcome them.

> While he [Jesus] was still speaking to the crowds, his mother and his brothers were standing outside, wanting to speak to him. Someone told him, "Look, your mother and your brothers are standing outside, wanting to speak to you." But to the one who had told him this, Jesus replied, "Who is my mother, and who are my brothers?" And pointing to his disciples, he said, "Here are my mother and my brothers! For whoever does the will of my Father in heaven is my brother and sister and mother."
>
> Matthew 12:46–50

When a woman in the crowd praised Jesus' mother and he replied, "Blessed rather are those who hear the word of God and obey it!" (Luke 11:28), Jesus was not only rejecting motherhood as the ultimate glory of a woman, but he was also casting doubts on his own mother's faithfulness to God.

No, Jesus was not close to his family, not at all.

Jesus' surprising teachings about families

Jesus was not "pro-family" in his teachings—not in the way we think of it, anyway. He never once told a parable about a married couple or about a mother and her children. In his most popular parable, that of the prodigal son, Jesus used the example of a dysfunctional family in order to teach about God's grace. At the age of twelve, he boldly told his parents, "I must be in my Father's house" (Luke 2:49)—and he was not referring to his parents' home! Jesus declared in no uncertain terms that his disciples must sever their own family ties in order to follow him:

> Jesus said, "Truly I tell you, there is no one who has left house or brothers or sisters or mother or father or children or fields, for my sake and for the sake of the good news, who will not receive a hundredfold now in this age—houses, brothers and sisters, mothers and children, and fields with persecutions— and in the age to come eternal life."
>
> Mark 10:29–30
> (compare Matthew 19:29 and Luke 18:29–30)

> For I have come to set a man against his father,
> and a daughter against her mother,
> and a daughter-in-law against her mother-in-law....
> Whoever loves father or mother more than me is not worthy of me; and whoever loves son or daughter more than me is not worthy of me...."
>
> Matthew 10:35, 37

> To another he said, "Follow me." But he said, "Lord, first let me go and bury my father." But Jesus said to him, "Let the dead bury their own dead; but as for you, go and proclaim the kingdom of God."
>
> Luke 9:59–60

> ...they will be divided:
>   father against son and son against father,
> mother against daughter
>   and daughter against mother,
> mother-in-law against her daughter-in-law
>   and daughter-in-law against mother-in-law.
>
> Luke 12:53

Jesus' call for his disciples to leave their families is presented in the harshest language of all in Luke's Gospel (Luke 14:26):

> Whoever comes to me and does not hate father and mother, wife and children, brothers and sisters, yes, and even life itself, cannot be my disciple.

Jesus promoted the breaking of family ties. Mark's Gospel presents the picture of James and John mending the nets of their family fishing business and then reports that "they left their father Zebedee in the boat with the hired men, and followed him." (Mark 1:20b) Jesus even insisted that his followers not even use the word *father* except in reference to God (Matthew 23:9).

In spite of Jesus' demand that his followers leave parents and siblings behind, Jesus provided for his own mother as he was dying on the cross (John 19:26–27), committing her to the care of one of his disciples. Moreover, Jesus condemned those who found loopholes in the law to avoid supporting their own parents (Mark 7:9–13a):

> Then he said to them, "You have a fine way of rejecting the commandment of God in order to keep your tradition! For Moses said, 'Honor your father and your mother'; and, 'Whoever speaks evil of father or mother must surely die.' But you say that if anyone tells father or mother, 'Whatever support you might have had from me is Corban' (that is, an offering to God)— then you no longer permit doing anything for a father or mother, thus making void the word of God through your tradition that you have handed on."

Jesus and children

In addition, Jesus strongly advocated children's rights—all children's rights, not just the eldest sons or those who happened to be born into a powerful family.

On one occasion a number of parents brought their children to Jesus so that he might lay his hands on them and bless them. This scene is often recalled during child dedication services or baptisms of infants.

People were bringing little children to him in order that he might touch them; and the disciples spoke sternly to them. But when Jesus saw this, he was indignant and said to them, "Let the little children come to me; do not stop them; for it is to such as these that the kingdom of God belongs. Truly I tell you, whoever does not receive the kingdom of God as a little child will never enter it." And he took them up in his arms, laid his hands on them, and blessed them.

Mark 10:13–16 (compare Matthew 19:13–14)

Casual readers often regard this event as a tender moment when Jesus expressed his love and appreciation for children. It is possible, however, that Jesus was trying to communicate a more pointed message. In his actions he may have been making a bold and radical statement about children.

Recall that a patriarch would lay his hands upon his eldest son's head and bestow upon him a blessing. The same words are used to describe Jesus' actions with these children: "he...laid his hands on them, and blessed them." The similarity of wording may be coincidental, but if it is not, then Jesus was bestowing something like the patriarchal blessing upon all of those children, all of them—eldest to youngest, boys and girls, none of whom were Jesus' own children!

If so, then Jesus was implying that every child is just as special as a firstborn son, that every child is blessed regardless of his or her family of origin, that every child is important, no matter how poor or humble his or her parents may be. By extension, he was saying that every family is important as well. This interpretation of Jesus' actions is consistent with his teachings about the value of children:

Truly I tell you, unless you change and become like children, you will never enter the kingdom of heaven. Whoever becomes humble like this child is the greatest in the kingdom of heaven. Whoever welcomes one such child in my name welcomes me.

Matthew 18:3–5

This interpretation would be consistent also with the forceful language that Jesus used in advocating children's rights:

> Whoever welcomes one such child in my name welcomes me. If any of you put a stumbling block before one of these little ones who believe in me, it would be better for you if a great millstone were fastened around your neck and you were drowned in the depth of the sea.
>
> Matthew 18:5–6

Moreover, it is likely that Jesus, by this action of blessing all sorts of children, was abolishing once and for all the patriarchal family system, with its favoritism toward the eldest male son, its strict rules on inheritance, and its stratification that favored some and disfranchised others.

In its place Jesus provided a new, extended family of God. Who are his own brothers and sisters and mother? They are any who do the will of his Father in heaven (Matthew 12:50). What happens when one leaves parents and siblings and children and lands to follow Jesus? He or she receives a hundred times as many in this age; and in the age to come, eternal life (Mark 10:29–30).

In a society where one's fate was largely determined by the wealth and status—or lack thereof—in one's family of origin, Jesus presented a radical new model of family life. The patriarch of this new family is God himself, our Father in heaven. All its members are to be regarded as children of God, even those who are of adult age according to the world's standards. Genetic family origins mean nothing, for all persons are equal in the eyes of our Father. All members are to care for one another as if they were biological brothers and sisters. Indeed, all members are linked together by "blood"—Christ's blood.

Inclusion in this family is possible only by the grace of God. Jesus could define this grace by using the example of a dysfunctional family in his parable of the prodigal son. In the close of the story, the father (representing God) reminds the firstborn son (who would be the favored one in the patriarchal family structure) that the younger son is "this brother of yours" (Luke 15:32).

The church as family

Jesus was certainly not "pro-family" in the usual sense of that term. Although he did not reject his family of origin, he insisted that his true family consisted of his devoted followers. ("Here are my mother and my brothers! For whoever does the will of my Father in heaven is my brother and sister and mother" [Matthew 12:49–50].)

Members of the early church apparently regarded themselves as Christ's family. They addressed each other as "sister" and "brother" (before these titles of affection became trite). By referring to each other this way, they were saying that they belonged to a new family, members together in the household of God.

Thus, the writer of Ephesians could speak of Christians as members of the same family and joint heirs:

> So then you are no longer strangers and aliens, but you are citizens with the saints and also members of the household of God....That is, the Gentiles have become fellow heirs, members of the same body, and sharers in the promise in Christ Jesus through the gospel.
>
> Ephesians 2:19; 3:6

Even a slave is to be considered a "beloved brother" to his master, according to Paul (Philemon 16)!

On the day of Pentecost this equality within the family of God was demonstrated in a dramatic way. One hundred and twenty disciples, both men and women, were "all" gathered in one place (Acts 1:14–15; 2:1). The sound of a violent wind filled "the entire house" (Acts 2:2), the tongues of fire rested on "each of them" (Acts 2:3), and they were "all" filled with the Spirit (Acts 2:4).

Casual readers of this passage often assume that only the twelve apostles were present and they only were filled with the Spirit. The author of Acts makes it clear, however, that all one hundred and twenty were recipients of the Spirit. Indeed, if it were otherwise Peter's interpretation of this spiritual event would not make sense. Instead of telling the amazed crowd in the street that the Spirit had come to a select number of male apostles, Peter quoted from the prophet Joel:

> In the last days it will be, God declares,
> that I will pour out my Spirit upon all flesh,
>   and your sons and your daughters shall prophesy,
> and your young men shall see visions,
>   and your old men shall dream dreams.
> Even upon my slaves, both men and women,
>   in those days I will pour out my Spirit,
>   and they shall prophesy.
>
> Acts 2:17–18

By lifting up this prophecy, Peter was not only providing a theological explanation for the remarkable fact that both men and women were filled with the Holy Spirit (a shocking thought within the Judaism of that time!), but he also was presenting a vision of a new order in which God's favor rests on all kinds of people—regardless of sex, age, or social status. Even slaves will be included in this divine commonwealth!

Later the apostle Paul echoed the experience of Pentecost in his famous dictum:

> There is no longer Jew or Greek, there is no longer slave or free, there is no longer male and female; for all of you are one in Christ Jesus.
>
> Galatians 3:28

All Christians are adopted into the family of God, he went on to say, and thus we all address God as "Abba! Father!" (Galatians 4:5–6).

Paul used other analogies to describe the oneness of Christians—branches on a tree (Romans 11:17–24), organs of a body (1 Corinthians 12:12–31 and elsewhere). But his favorite title for Christians was *adelphoi*, "brothers and sisters."[3]

In 2 Timothy 1:1–7, Paul (or, as many scholars assume, one who used Paul's name) addressed Timothy in ways that illustrate the concept of spiritual family.

He referred to Timothy as "my beloved child" (verse 2), even though they were not biologically related. Paul went on to say that he thanked God night and day for Timothy (verse 3). Recalling young Timothy's tears, Paul expressed a longing to see him and thereby to be "filled with joy" (verse 4). Paul then praised Timothy's faith, tracing its descent through Timothy's grandmother and mother (verse 5). Then Paul encouraged and challenged Timothy to rekindle his God-given gift, in a spirit of power and love and self-discipline (verses 6–7).

Although the form of this letter is typical of first-century epistles in general, its tone is that of a caring family member. In contrast to the attitude of many adults toward youth who are not related to them, Paul told young Timothy that he was loved, wanted, and needed. The words warmly reflect a sense of belonging to a supportive family, the extended family of God.

The early church also included a number of widows—women without families—and gave them special honor and opportunities for service (compare Acts 6:1; 1 Timothy 5:3; James 1:27). After the close of the New Testament era, the writings of Polycarp and Tertullian, as well as various church manuals, report that widows were cared for and honored. They were often seated in front of the congregation near the altar. In the same way care was extended to orphans and abandoned children, to the extent that Christians in Rome would often take newborn infants who had been left to die of exposure and rear them as their own.

According to ancient rabbinical thought, it is the duty of every man to father children. A male was not even regarded as a man until he had sired a child, and barrenness itself was named as grounds for divorce. To fail to produce children was considered the same as murder in the thought of some rabbis. "If you have no descendants," one rabbi asked, "upon whom will the *Shekhinah* [God's glory] rest? Upon trees and stones?"

We find no such demand that marriages produce children in the teachings of Jesus and of Paul. Instead, all kinds of persons are invited to enter into an extended family, in which Jesus is the firstborn Son and all others are equal. In this family no one is to be addressed as "father" (Matthew 23:9). Instead, all learn to address God as "Abba"—the Aramaic equivalent of "Daddy"—and regard one another as brothers and sisters.

Although the New Testament epistles portray the church as an extended family, it was nonetheless filled with family units, and in two of the letters (both attributed to Paul) the relationship of parent and child is addressed:

> Children, obey your parents in the Lord, for this is right. "Honor your father and mother"—this is the first commandment with a promise: "so that it may be well with you and you may live long on the earth."
>
> And, fathers, do not provoke your children to anger, but bring them up in the discipline and instruction of the Lord.
>
> Ephesians 6:1–4
>
> Children, obey your parents in everything, for this is your acceptable duty in the Lord. Fathers, do not provoke your children, or they may lose heart.
>
> Colossians 3:20–21

These parallel passages are designed to complement the fifth of the Ten Commandments: "Honor your father and your mother" (Exodus 20:12). In both Ephesians and Colossians the imperative that children "honor" their parents is translated into the more specific directive, "obey." However, both writings also complement this commandment with an injunction directed at parents: "do not provoke your children...."

Two different words in these passages are both translated "provoke." In the Ephesians letter the word is *parorgizo* (par-or-GEEZ-o). It simply means "make angry." By using this word, the writer was urging parents not to infuriate their children. Instead, according to the English version, parents are to "bring them up in the discipline and instruction of the Lord." The word for "bring up" is *ektrepho* (ek-TREF-o). It refers to rearing children, but the word is rich with positive feeling, conveying the additional meanings of nurturing and cherishing.

The Colossians passage differs in emphasis. The word translated "provoke" in that writing is *erethizo* (er-eth-EEZ-o), which means to arouse, to irritate, even to embitter. It is a coarse word that might better be rendered by our idiomatic term "bitch." The other special word in that same sentence is *athumeo* (ah-thu-MEH-o), to lose heart or become discouraged. This term implies an attitude of one who has lost hope and is depressed.

The writer to the Colossian Christians, then, is pleading with parents not to "bitch" at their children, lest their offspring become so discouraged that they give up.

Implications from the New Testament view of families

If we are to take the New Testament view of family seriously, then we will not assume that all families are of positive value, either to their own members or to society as a whole. We will regard single individuals, childless couples, and children of broken homes as of equal worth to those who constitute "families." We will not glorify "the family pew," but instead seek to form the congregation into an extended family for all its members.

Notes

[1] Compare Exodus 21:17: "Whoever curses father or mother shall be put to death."

[2] One exception to this prohibition is Jephthah's offering of his daughter (Judges 11). Some scholars have argued that he simply sent her to a kind of convent, in the way that Hannah gave her son to Eli, the priest. Other examples of child sacrifice were regarded with horror and disgust by the Hebrews (cf. 2 Kings 3:27; 6:24–31; 16:3; 17:17)

[3] *Adelphoi* literally means "brothers," but since the masculine ending can also be gender-indefinite, *adelphoi* can indicate both brothers and sisters.

Questions for Discussion

1. Consider three concepts of "family": the patriarchal *bet-'ab* in ancient Israel, the household of God in the early church, and the nuclear family in modern Western society. Which of these three would provide the best support for its members? The greatest safeguard against sexual or physical abuse? The most individual freedom?

2. Although Jesus insisted that his followers must be willing to leave their families, many churches affirm the value of strong family ties. Are these churches thereby denying the gospel? Why or why not?

3. Some churches attempt to control the thoughts and choices of their members and justify this effort by stating that the church is "family." How much individual freedom must Christians give up in order to be "one body" and "the household of God"?

4. Why has the traditional understanding of the Pentecost event focused upon the speaking in tongues, rather than upon the meaning given to it by Peter himself during his sermon?

5. In what ways is it possible for a church to become an extended family? For a church to provide support for children of nonmembers?

10

Biblical Insights
About Relationships

The primary purpose of the Bible is to build relationships. The Hebrew prophets continually called the people of Israel back to their covenantal relationship with God, including its demand for justice and mercy between people. Jesus summarized the law of Moses in terms of two relationships, love of God and love of neighbor.

Although certain scripture passages focus on the specific relationships of marriages and of family life, many other passages address the problems of more general relationships. Large portions of the New Testament epistles, for example, are concerned with the extended Christian family, the church. However, these same texts are as applicable and valuable for the home as they

135

are for the congregation. For this reason, families can enrich their own relationships by reading such passages together and then reflecting on ways that these teachings might enrich their own life together.

Such passages of scripture that are so numerous, however, that simply quoting such texts, without even providing commentary, would fill many hundreds of pages! Instead, I will identify three difficult passages that provide helpful insights about broken relationships and healthy self-esteem, but are often misunderstood.

Hurts and resentments

Since the greatest hurts can come from those whom we love the most, scriptures that pertain to resentments may be especially relevant for married couples and family members.

The model prayer of Jesus (usually referred to as "The Lord's Prayer" or "The 'Our Father'") contains a very unusual petition: "And forgive us our debts, /as we also have forgiven our debtors" (Matthew 6:12). The wording of the prayer in Luke's Gospel is somewhat different: "And forgive us our sins, /for we ourselves forgive everyone indebted to us" (Luke 11:4a).

In our own culture we often hear the advice, "forgive and forget." Sometimes, however, when a hurt reaches deep into one's memory, forgiveness is difficult and forgetting is virtually impossible. A well-wisher who recommends that the victim of a grave sin simply "forgive and forget" is really asking that person to deny the seriousness of the offense and to treat it as a minor inconvenience.

Not only are such sentiments a source of frustration for the one who is bearing a resentment, but the warning that follows Jesus' prayer (in Matthew) seems to make "forgiving and forgetting" a requirement for the victim's own salvation:

> For if you forgive others their trespasses, your heavenly
> Father will also forgive you; but if you do not forgive
> others, neither will your Father forgive your trespasses.
>   Matthew 6:14–15

Both Matthew and Luke's versions speak of sins as if they were debts that are owed by the sinner. Moreover, the word that is translated "forgive" literally means "release"—as in writing off a debt. This was the way that Jews in the first century spoke of wrongs, as debts that are incurred.

Behind this linguistic metaphor lies a wonderfully wise understanding about resentments. Referring to wrongs done to a person as "debts" affirms the seriousness of the offense and the reality of its lingering effect upon the recipient. It implies that stealing even something as intangible as peace of mind is nonetheless a theft. Jesus never belittled an emotional loss as insignificant. He never asked his followers to become too tough to care about any hurts they might receive.

Instead, Jesus implied that a person who has mistreated another is in that person's debt. Saying this affirms the reality of a victim's emotional response.

Jesus' next words, however, assert that a person who has been hurt by another can deliberately choose to cancel the debt that his or her offender owes. He or she is not asked to "forgive and forget," but to "release." Doing this is an act of grace, of unmerited mercy, on the part of the victim that does not denigrate the offense or depend upon any change of heart by the offender. Releasing the debt gives the one who has been hurt a sense of choice and control.

The postscript to Jesus' model prayer ("For if you forgive others their trespasses, your heavenly Father will also forgive you….") provides an additional incentive to cancel the moral and spiritual indebtedness of others. Jesus' words remind us that our relationship with anyone who has hurt us does effect our spiritual relationship with God. The two are interconnected.

Jesus attested (according to Matthew) that our relationship with God and our relationships with others are interconnected:

> When the Pharisees heard that he had silenced the Sadducees, they gathered together, and one of them, a lawyer, asked him a question to test him. "Teacher, which commandment in the law is the greatest?" He said to him, "'You shall love the

Lord your God with all your heart, and with all your soul, and with all your mind.' This is the greatest and first commandment. And a second is like it: 'You shall love your neighbor as yourself.' On these two commandments hang all the law and the prophets."

Matthew 22:34–40

Jesus paired these two commandments, even though they are drawn from widely separate portions of the Pentateuch. The second one "is like" the first. Elsewhere Jesus illustrated how our relationship with other people is to be based on God's relationship with us:

You have heard that it was said, "You shall love your neighbor and hate your enemy." But I say to you, Love your enemies and pray for those who persecute you, so that you may be children of your Father in heaven; for he makes his sun rise on the evil and on the good, and sends rain on the righteous and on the unrighteous.

Matthew 5:43–45

It is written in the prophets, "And they shall all be taught by God." Everyone who has heard and learned from the Father comes to me.

John 6:45

Reconciliation

According to the Gospel of Matthew (18:15–20), Jesus spelled out specific steps that a person who has been hurt is to take. However, these instructions are often misunderstood:

If your brother* sins against you, go and point out the fault when the two of you are alone. If the member listens to you, you have regained that one.† But if you are not listened to, take one or two others along with you, so that every word may be confirmed by the evidence of two or three witnesses.

*The NRSV actually renders this as "If another member of the church…," with "your brother" referenced as a more accurate translation of the Greek.
†The Greek reads "the brother."

If the member refuses to listen to them, tell it to the church; and if the offender refuses to listen even to the church, let such a one be to you as a Gentile and a tax collector. Truly I tell you, whatever you bind on earth will be bound in heaven, and whatever you loose on earth will be loosed in heaven. Again, truly I tell you, if two of you agree on earth about anything you ask, it will be done for you by my Father in heaven. For where two or three are gathered in my name, I am there among them."

It may not be an accident that a passage concerning reconciliation begins with the phrase, "If your brother...." The relationships that matter most are those we have with family members, whether the family be that of our own household or the extended family of a church.

The English translation of verse 15 is unfortunate, in that the instruction—"point out the fault" of another—sounds as if Christ has commissioned his followers to become fault-finders. The goal of this teaching, however, is not for persons to identify the failings of others, but to achieve reconciliation between those who have been estranged. The words translated "point out the fault" mean that reconciliation begins when we can honestly identify the real source of our contention.

The series of steps to be taken in an effort to heal a broken relationship seems clear, beginning with a private meeting and, if need be, ending by taking the matter before the *ekklesia* (eklay-SEE-ah). *Ekklesia* was a common word, meaning an assembly of people. In the New Testament, *ekklesia* is normally translated as "church," and it is likely that this is what the Gospel writer had in mind. But if Jesus himself really did use this word before his death and resurrection, then he was probably referring to a general gathering of his disciples.[1]

These instructions run counter to our normal way of reacting to an offense. Most people prefer to skip the first step, that of a private meeting, or any face-to-face encounter at all! Instead, most persons want to tell others, to gain sympathy, to seek revenge by reporting the other person's wrongdoing. However, this passage will not let us indulge ourselves in mouth-to-ear retaliation. We may tell our story to others only after a private conference has failed, and even then we may do so only as an honest attempt to establish peace.

Not until the church has tried to mediate and failed may we treat the wrongdoer "as a Gentile and a tax collector." This phrase sounds as if Jesus was giving his disciples permission to shun offenders. That may have been the intention; however, it is also possible that by choosing these words Jesus was saying something like this: "Treat the person as one who is in need of forgiveness, but has not yet heard the good news of God's love and grace."

The seriousness of this passage is emphasized by the words in verse 18: "Truly I tell you, whatever you bind on earth will be bound in heaven, and whatever you loose on earth will be loosed in heaven." The state of our relationships on earth will be mirrored in eternity.

Ministers often quote the last verse (20) of this passage on those occasions when church attendance is slack: "For where two or three are gathered in my name, I am there among them." These words were not penned by the Gospel writer, however, in order to provide a blessing for small numbers! The word that is translated "gathered" conveys the image of bringing together people who were once estranged from one another. The theme of the whole passage, then, is reiterated once more, as Christ promises to be present whenever reconciliation takes place.

The nature of humility

Some parents are generous in praising their children, fearing that without it their offspring might lack self-confidence and a sense of personal worth. Other parents refrain from giving words of praise to their children (or to their spouses, for that matter), fearing that doing so will give them a false sense of their own importance and make them disagreeably haughty. After all, humility is a virtue, and one ought not to think too highly of oneself.

Those who hold to this notion about the dangers of praise sometimes quote Philippians 2:3 as their authority: "Do nothing from selfish ambition or conceit, but in humility regard others as better than yourselves."

Many religious folk teach their children and others the so-called "JOY" formula for humility: "Put *Jesus* first, *Others* second, and *Yourself* third." Others argue that teaching children to regard other persons as more important or better than themselves is unhealthy, in that it fosters a timid and self-deprecating spirit and leaves them emotionally defenseless against verbal or sexual abuse.

The context of this scripture quotation is Paul's letter to his "brothers and sisters" in Philippi, a congregation that had shown concern for him as he lingered in prison. Apparently some Christians had used Paul's imprisonment as a means of boasting (1:17), while others are wondering how such a respected leader could end up behind bars. Paul assured them that his humble situation is actually furthering the preaching of the gospel (1:12–14). He then offered a theological basis for the true nature of humility (Philippians 2:1–11):

> If then there is any encouragement in Christ, any consolation from love, any sharing in the Spirit, any compassion and sympathy, make my joy complete: be of the same mind, having the same love, being in full accord and of one mind. Do nothing from selfish ambition or conceit, but in humility regard others as better than yourselves. Let each of you look not to your own interests, but to the interests of others. Let the same mind be in you that was in Christ Jesus,
> who, though he was in the form of God,
> did not regard equality with God
> as something to be exploited,
> but emptied himself,
> taking the form of a slave,
> being born in human likeness.
> And being found in human form,
> he humbled himself

and became obedient to the point of death—
even death on a cross.

Therefore God also highly exalted him
and gave him the name
that is above every name,
so that at the name of Jesus
every knee should bend,
in heaven and on earth and under the earth,
and every tongue should confess
that Jesus Christ is Lord,
to the glory of God the Father.

At first glance, Paul's words might seem designed to produce the greatest sense of inferiority imaginable in his readers! Not only is one to refrain from doing anything that is self-rewarding, not only is one to regard himself or herself as inferior to all others, but the reader is even urged to imitate Christ himself—who gave up equality with God and was executed on a cross!

Moreover, Paul also seems to have encouraged his fellow Christians to become busybodies, telling them, "Let each of you look not to your own interests, but to the interests of others." Taking his words literally would be futile. How can a group of people all be of one mind, each regarding all the others as better than himself or herself, all persons doing only what all the others want?

Let us remember that Paul was addressing a specific problem. Some members of the congregation at Philippi regarded themselves as better than Paul because they had not experienced his misfortune of being imprisoned. Behind that attitude lay the smug notion that troubles come only to those individuals who are bad or stupid.

So Paul crafted his response carefully. He reminded them that Christ himself was once a prisoner, that Christ was even tortured to death—and in a manner reserved for the vilest of criminals. Moreover, Christ actually chose this fate, taking "the form of a slave" and humbling himself. Because Christ so humbled himself on behalf of others, God has bestowed upon him "the name /that is above all names."

By appealing to the example of Christ, Paul has identified the true nature of humility: service to others. And by appealing to the example of Christ, Paul has identified the source of true greatness: God's approval.

If we are to listen to this passage carefully and convey its wisdom to our children, perhaps we might teach them something like this: humility is not just attitude but action—it is serving others rather than being served. Greatness is acheived, not by being admired by others or even thinking well of ourselves, but by pleasing God.

Applying scriptures to marriage and family life

Many other biblical passages offer helpful wisdom and encouragement for married couples and families. A fun and helpful use of scriptures involves restating the principles found within the text, only in the context of modern home life.

Here is one delightful example of that use of the Bible, in which my wife rewrote portions of the Sermon on the Mount to apply specifically to the daily interactions of parents and children:

THE SERMON ON THE RUG
by Christy Bristow

After calling the family together, he sat down on the rug in the midst of them, and opened his mouth and taught them, saying:

Blessed are you when you contribute to your family either in service or in the fruit of your occupation, for you shall be rewarded.

Blessed are you when you comfort a family member who is hurting, or care for one who is sick, for family members are God's children, and serving them is serving God.

Blessed are those who are willing to do a little more than their fair share, for they keep family life agreeable.

Blessed are those who keep discussions from becoming arguments and can resist raising their voice, for peace keepers are loved of God.

Blessed are ones who care for the family pets, for pets are also God's creatures and they give much love to those who love them.

Blessed are those who clean up after themselves and see that their duties are accomplished at the appropriate time, thereby not tempting others to fall into nagging and fussing, for they shall not receive nagging and fussing.

Blessed are you who honor your family members as you honor your friends. When you honor them during the difficult times, when sickness comes, during holidays, when guests overstay, when money is not to be found in your house, when other relatives are being difficult, your reward will be great, for you shall find stress can push you closer together and you will be a stronger family than you were before.

Anyone who nurses strife and dissension shall reap the fruits along with the whole family. If you are preparing for worship and realize that your child or your spouse has reason to have a grudge against you, make peace within the family unit before you attend worship, and then make your offering a thank-offering for your forgiveness and the gift of your family.

If a family member accuses you, do not be too quick to deny or to shift the blame, but deal with the problem directly and avoid game-playing.

Be loyal to your family members. Do not hold them up unfavorably either publicly or privately. Do not compare them unfavorably to another, saying, "Why can't you be more like your brother?" or, "My mother always ironed the sheets!" for leading a child of God to think poorly of himself or herself is a grievous sin. Instead, practice rejoicing in the strengths and uniqueness of your family members.

Keep your promises and fulfill what you say you will do, even if a friend invites you to something more interesting, for not honoring your commitments creates hurt feelings and anxiety within the family.

You have heard it said, "If your brother hits you, hit him back!" and, "Sticks and stones may break my bones, but names will never hurt me." But I say to you, do not fight or argue with your family. If your mother tells you to hang up your coat, hang up your sibling's coat as well. If your father tells you to mow the lawn, sweep the grass off the sidewalk as well. If your sister or daughter wants to wear your sweater, offer her the shirt that goes with it.

You have heard it said, "Be polite to company and use your best table manners when you are a guest in someone's home."

But I say to you: treat your spouse and children or your siblings and parents with all the courtesy you use with your friends. If you are pleasant only to those who are always pleasant to you, what reward can you expect? Anyone can be pleasant under those conditions! Go into your own home, shut the door, and practice your charm and consideration on your own family, who have the most opportunity to irritate you regularly.

You must forgive relatives their irritating habits, for if you forgive them their faults, they will find it much easier to forgive you yours.

And when you diet, do not assume a crabby countenance and sullen disposition or people will sabotage your effort and you will not receive the reward of a slender body.

Remember always that your spouse, your children, your parents, your siblings, and all your other relatives are God's children and are to be treated as such. By doing so, even when they are not acting like God's children, you will help remind them of their holiness, and help bring them back to behavior appropriate to a child of God.[2]

Notes

[1]Many New Testament scholars have concluded that Jesus did not say the things attributed to him in this passage, because the church did not come into existence until after Jesus' earthly ministry and therefore Jesus would not have told his followers to "tell it to the church" (verse 17a).   However, the instruction "let such a one be to you as a Gentile and a tax collector" (verse 17b) is Judean in character and reflects a social setting from before the destruction of Jerusalem (A.D. 70).   It is unlikely that this phrase would be chosen by an evangelist whose Gospel concludes with the Great Commission to all the world (Matthew 28:19), and it would be especially ironic for it to appear in the first Gospel, which came to be attributed to an apostle who was once a tax collector.

[2]Christy Bristow, "Sermon on the Rug," copyright 1979.   Used by permission.

Questions for Discussion

1. Can you think of other metaphors for trespasses besides "debts" that will faciliate a healthy response to resentments?

2. Consider the four steps recommended in Matthew 18:15–20 for one who has been hurt. How might these efforts be regarded from the point of the person who is accused of having been hurtful?

3. To what extent do our interpersonal relationships effect our spiritual relationship with God, and vice versa?

4. What might be the attitude of modern Christians whose leader, like the apostle Paul, was sentenced to prison?

5. Paul often compared the church to a body, with the individual members having differing gifts, all of which are necessary for the body to live and function. To what extent is this metaphor helpful in the matter of self-conceit and humility?

Appendix:
Marriage in Eternity?

Sadducees, members of a sect within Judaism during the first century of this era, were biblical literalists. Because they did not find any direct statement in the Pentateuch about a resurrection of the dead, they did not believe that there was any life after death.

A number of Sadducees decided to ask Jesus a difficult question, one designed to show the impossibility of the resurrection of the dead. They invented a scenario in which a woman was married to seven brothers, one after the other, in the custom of levirate marriages. (See Chapter 2.) Then these Sadducees (who did not believe in the resurrection of the dead) asked Jesus a clever question: "In the resurrection, therefore, whose wife will the woman be?"

The incident is recorded in all three of the synoptic Gospels (Matthew, Mark, and Luke). Luke reports it this way (20:27–36; compare Matthew 22:23–30 and Mark 12:18–25):

> Some Sadducees, those who say there is no resurrection, came to him and asked him a question, "Teacher, Moses wrote for us that if a man's brother dies, leaving a wife but no children, the man shall marry the widow and raise up children for his brother. Now there were seven brothers; the first married, and died childless; then the second and the third married her, and so in the same way all seven died childless. Finally the woman also died. In the resurrection, therefore, whose wife will the woman be? For the seven had married her."

> Jesus said to them, "Those who belong to this age marry and are given in marriage; but those who are considered worthy of a place in that age and in the resurrection from the dead neither marry nor are given in marriage. Indeed they cannot die anymore, because they are like angels and are children of God, being children of the resurrection."

The portion of Jesus' reply found within verse 36 challenged three popular assumptions about marriage and about life after death.

First, Jesus declared that there is no need for marriage in the life to come. People in this age marry, but people in the age to come do not marry. Why would they not marry? Jesus put it simply: "they cannot die anymore." Therefore, they would have no reason to get married.

The purpose for marriage, according to the society in which Jesus lived, was to produce children. One rabbi questioned what would happen if a generation did not produce children. "Upon what would God's glory rest," he asked, "upon rocks and trees?" In other words, we get married in order to have children in order to perpetuate the human race after we are dead.

Jesus stated, however, that after the resurrection people will never die again; hence, they will not need to bear children.

Nowhere else did Jesus did give voice to the idea that the purpose of marriage was to produce children. Instead, he argued that the goal of marriage is for a couple to become "one flesh." (See Chapter 4.) God saw that Adam was all alone and needed someone who was nice and soft and friendly, and so God created Eve. Therefore the purpose of marriage, from the very beginning, in the mind of God, has been companionship.

However, since the Sadducees and most others within first-century Judea believed that the purpose of marriage was to produce children, Jesus pointed out that in the afterlife that purpose would no longer exist. Hence, there would be no need for marriage. Jesus turned their own perceptions about marriage against them.

Second, Jesus explained that in the resurrection people will not have physical bodies. Instead, they will be like angels (verse 36). This must have surprised his listeners, because most people in that society believed that at the resurrection God would somehow re-create our physical bodies. Not so, Jesus told them. We will be like the angels, those messengers from God who seem to be able to appear suddenly when needed.

Third, Jesus stated that those who are resurrected will be "children of God" (verse 36). If that phrase meant anything, it surely meant that such persons will belong to God. As the author of Revelation later worded it (21:3–4),

And I heard a loud voice from the throne saying,
    "See, the home of God is among mortals.
    He will dwell with them;
    they will be his peoples,
    and God himself will be with them;
    he will wipe every tear from their eyes.
    Death will be no more;
    mourning and crying and pain will be no more,
    for the first things have passed away."

It is possible that Jesus, by stating that those in the age to come will be God's children, is gently suggesting to the Sadducees that God will not let his children die eternally. But the phrase "children of God" used in this context may have had a more pointed purpose.

It may be that by using this phrase Jesus was identifying the attitude of those who are "worthy" of the resurrection. He had already stated that no one can enter the kingdom of God unless he or she becomes as a little child. (Matthew 18:3; compare Mark 10:15 and Luke 18:17). By declaring that those who are resurrected will be "children of God," Jesus may have been describing the attitude of those who will enjoy the afterlife.

Or, it may be that Jesus was identifying an equality among those who are "worthy" of the resurrection. The phrase itself literally reads "sons of God," but it is quite unlikely that Jesus believed only males would be resurrected. In Judean society (and elsewhere in the ancient world), however, sons were favored over daughters. By referring to all who are resurrected as "sons," it may mean that Jesus was implying that all persons in the age to come will enjoy equal value. Women will not be relegated to a second class status in the resurrection. The word *sons* in this phrase may indicate not sexual exclusion, but social equality.

Or, it may be that Jesus was identifying the companionship that will be enjoyed by those who are "worthy" of the resurrection. Perhaps he was saying that in the world to come the need for companionship will be fulfilled in ways that even the best of marriages cannot do.

However these words are interpreted, this passage of scripture clearly asserts that marriage will not exist in the afterlife.

Index